The Yoginis of Ranipur Jharial :
Tantric Goddesses of Yore

The Yoginis of Ranipur Jharial : Tantric Goddesses of Yore

Dr. Adyasha Das

BLACK EAGLE BOOKS
2021

BLACK EAGLE BOOKS

USA address:
7464 Wisdom Lane
Dublin, OH 43016

India address:
E/312, Trident Galaxy, Kalinga Nagar,
Bhubaneswar-751003, Odisha, India

E-mail: info@blackeaglebooks.org
Website: www.blackeaglebooks.org

First International Edition Published by
BLACK EAGLE BOOKS, 2021

The Yoginis of Ranipur Jharial : Tantric Goddesses of Yore
by **Dr. Adyasha Das**

Copyright © **Dr. Adyasha Das**

All rights reserved. No part of this publication may be reproduced, stored in a retrieval system, or transmitted, in any form or by any means, electronic, mechanical, photocopying, recording or otherwise without the prior permission of the publisher.

Cover Photo : **Siddhartha Sanjib**
Cover & Interior Design: Ezy's Publication

ISBN- 978-1-64560-210-1 (Paperback)
Library of Congress Control Number: 2021945701

Printed in the United States of America

Contents

Preface 7

Introduction: The Mysterious Yoginis 13

The Yogini Temples: Past and Present-
an overview of Yogini Temples in India 32

Ranipur Jharial
The Abode of the Chausathi Yoginis 50

Getting to know the Yoginis of Ranipur Jharial 66

Ancient Temples of Ranipur Jharial 88

The untapped tourism potential of Ranipur Jharial 101

PREFACE

My tryst with the Yoginis began when I got a training assignment at Hirapur, a nondescript village near Bhubaneswar where the relatively unknown Chausathi Yogini Temple is located. I did not realize then that I was stepping into a passion that would deeply connect me to the elusive Yoginis. This interest spurred not only my readings but also my travels in Odisha and all over the country, even foreign lands in the trail of the Yoginis. From Hirapur, Ranipur Jharial, Khajuraho, Morena and other lost yogini temples scattered in India to Cambodia and Indonesia, I have met the Yoginis everywhere. Visiting the abode of the Yoginis was an intensely spiritual experience for me, a transcendental experience.

Initially I started with a project dedicated to the Yoginis of Hirapur, musically expressing my long-standing tryst with the Chausathi Yoginis, to be presented to them in the form of a song. The song took shape bit by bit, beginning under the patch of blue sky we could see from where we stood inside the hypaethral temple of Hirapur, the abode of the Yoginis. The melody weaves the texture of a trance, helping in deepening the listener's insight. The use of traditional, authentic musical instruments further accentuated the experience. The vocal melody, mantric utterance, and rhythmic flow were enmeshed to create the mysticism of the Yoginis.

Immediately after this, the book I had planned about the Yoginis of Hirapur took shape. Based on my research, readings and information which I collected from museums in several places, local historians and heritage specialists, I tried to demystify the relatively unknown Chausathi Yoginis of Hirapur. Several rare aspects of this temple intrigued me. The Yogini cult, tantric in nature and Tantra itself, projecting the efficacy of magical rituals and spells, sounds and gestures, is intertwined deeply with rural and tribal traditions. There is a diverse range of attitudes toward the tantric traditions, ranging from viewing it as a path of liberation to the relatively widespread associations of the tantric traditions with sorcery and libertine sexuality. In Hinduism, the tantric tradition is most often associated with its goddess tradition called Shaktism, followed by Shaivism and Vaishnavism. In this temple, every male deity except Shiva are replaced by a female counterpart including Ganesha, all of them representing varied qualities. The Yoginis were believed to impart magical powers to their worshippers.

Amidst the panoramic beauty of the villages in Odisha, there are countless temples housing gramadevatis. The sacred place of worship of the Hindus is the temple or devalaya, the house of the God. A temple is a space, a structure for various religious activities. It is a place of community worship, of communication between gods and devotees. The temples also serve as a promoter of the arts, a place for divine experience, entertainment, aesthetic relish, social togetherness, as well as home for artistes in the fields of sculpture, painting, music, dance and philosophy.

The Yogini
I would know her anywhere
A wild tangled forest
Of mysteries, temples and treasures within!

My growing interest in the Yoginis led me to the study of the intriguing world of Tantra. The Sanskrit word 'Tantra' derives from the root Tan, etymologically meaning 'to weave' or 'compose'. "Tannat Trayate Iti Tantra" - This means the body is used to swim across the body (literally that which makes one swim across the body). Mantra makes one swim across the mind (Man; Mind) and Yantra makes one swim across forms (Yan : Form).

Tan: Body, Tra: to swim across, Ta : other, Na : is not

All these four words are packed into Tantra, meaning the body is used as if it is not the body to transcend the body- "Pravritti pathe Nivritti"

Tantra denotes the esoteric traditions of Hinduism and Buddhism that developed in India from the middle of the 1st millennium CE onwards. Tantra in the Indian tradition also means any systematic, broadly applicable text, theory, system, method, instrument, technique or practice. A key feature of these traditions is the use of mantras, and thus they are commonly referred to as Mantramarga (Path of Mantra) in Hinduism or Mantrayana (Mantra Vehicle) and Guhyamantra (Secret Mantra) in Buddhism. in the Ranipur Jharial site itself there is evidence of prominent Yantra(s) in the rocky outcrop in the vicinity of the Yogini Temple. Tantra has continuously and consistently challenged the fundamentals of religion, culture and politics around the world. The Tantric worldview interprets material reality as animated by Shakti – unlimited, divine feminine power. Tantric goddesses challenged traditional models of womanhood as passive and docile in their intertwining of aggressive and erotic power.

My book *"The Chausathi Yoginis of Hirapur: from Tantra to Tourism"*, which went on to become the Amazon Bestseller several times was appreciated by my readers. As a teacher of Tourism and a trainer of human resources in the tourism industry, it gave me immense satisfaction that the book was well received by the tourism fraternity. The Yoginis aroused in me great inspiration, their greatness breathing poetry into me. Encounters with them made me realize that the world's most valuable resource is love, that God is a woman, that the mystery of the Yoginis was decipherable by allocations of time, situation, and perspective. These led me to write a series of poems which led to the publication of the anthology, "The Yogini Poems: Love and Life". These poems are a tribute to the forgotten Yoginis and are an attempt to write about the silence, light and space in the life and love meanderings of the Yogini. The demure Yoginis of Hirapur had enthralled me but I was equally interested in the mysterious Yoginis of Ranipur Jharial, the second Yogini temple in Odisha. The cluster of temples nestling in the twin villages of Ranipur and Jharial at Bolangir, Odisha was archaeologically, historically and religiously significant.

The Mysterious Yoginis of Ranipur Jharial

During my visit to the site and later my readings into this hypaethral temple, I found the location of the temple and the sculptures intriguing – a great number of animal-headed Yoginis, some clearly distinguishable like the one with a cat head, or an elephant head. The images of the goddesses are large in comparison to the petite sculptures at the Hirapur temple, but with prominent physical features. All the Yoginis are shown dancing, each striking an identical pose. The positioning of the legs and at times hands is very similar to the Odissi dance form. This interest led to the creation of this book, "**The Yoginis of Ranipur Jharial : Tantric Goddesses of Yore**".

Representing one of the most astounding affiliates of Tantra which connected various strands of incompatible religious traditions, it appeared that the Yoginis communicated with a visual language of their own. The mysteries of the elusive Yoginis at Ranipur Jharial lie in the ferocious, untamed female whose body transmits the power of life. Shakti is a shifting network or chain of relations, emanating from all parts of the cosmos and the social organism, and is focused above all in the human body and sexuality (Urban 2001: 785).

I thank Satya Pattanaik, Director, Black Eagle Books, USA for supporting the publication of this book. He has also published my previous two books on the Yoginis and extended his unstinted support for their sustained promotion. I extend my thanks to Ashok Parida, BEB for a beautiful cover design and lay-out. My thanks goes to Sankar Narayan Mallik, who has rendered invaluable help and his expertise in reading the manuscript thoroughly and providing indispensable editorial insights. His knowledge, experience and perspective has enriched the book. I thank him for his co-operation in my literary endeavours.

My family, Lalit and Ishani, share my interest for travel and literature and most of these visits to the Yogini circuits have been with them. Had it not been for them, I may not have seen so many beautiful destinations. As a senior police officer, my husband, Lalit Das, ADG, Police, Govt. of Odisha had friends at all these far-flung destinations who have rendered invaluable help to me in the process of my research. Special thanks to my mother, Pratibha Ray, who is in the truest sense, a friend, philosopher and guide, and has been a constructive critic at all times. As a writer herself, my discussions with her in the course of my research and writings were very helpful to me. My sincere thanks to Sri Kusalkar Nitin Dagudu, Superintendent of Police, Bolangir for his assistance in getting access to rare books and photographs on the Yoginis of Ranipur Jharial. My thanks also go to Nanda Kishore Behera and Siddhartha Sanjib for providing me with rare and creative photographs of the destination. The interest and appreciation of my readers made me contemplate the idea of putting together my insights in the form of a book. I remain indebted to them.

The Yogini cult extolled women as rendering dominant roles in leadership and creative inventions of an ancient culture. Mostly, I pay reverence to the unseen force which made me know the world in myself through these visits to the Yogini temple.

Introduction:
The Mysterious Yoginis

The cult of the Chausathi (sixty-four) Yoginis was at a time widely prevalent in the central and eastern parts of India along with other cults of Shakta-tantrism.

The culture of sixty-four Yoginis was the exuberant expression of an extreme form of tantrism in about 8th century A.D. when the occult and esoteric Sadhana reached the highest peak. The origin of the pantheon of sixty-four yoginis is shrouded in mystery. The vedic and post-vedic literature mention the names of some individual yoginis, but never sixty-four manifestations together. Through the process of transformation, the cult came into existence and exerted an important niche in the Shakta-tantric pantheon. The puranas and Upa-puranas which are the source of different cults are referred to find out the origin of sixty-four yoginis, who are basically the mother-goddesses. (Origin of Tantrism and Sixty-Four Yogini Cult in Orissa - Dr. Janmejay Choudhury)

The Shakti cult came into prominence during the period of Shankaracharya, around 9th Century AD. There are five major shrines of the Sixty-four Yoginis (Chausathi

Yogini, among other spellings) in India (named for 64 legendary yoginis), two in Odisha and three in Madhya Pradesh. One of the most impressive yogini temples in Odisha is the ninth century CE hypaethral Chausathi Yogini Temple located at Hirapur in Khurda district, 15 km south of Bhubaneshwar. Another hypaethral sixty-four yogini temple in Odisha is the Chausathi Yogini Pitha in Ranipur-Jharial, near Titilagarh in Balangir district. Few images of the Sixty-four Yoginis are missing from this temple.

Two notable yogini temples in Madhya Pradesh are the ninth-century Chaunsath Yogini Temple to the southwest of the western group of temples in Khajuraho, near Chhatarpur in Chhatarpur District, and the 10th century CE Chaunsath Yogini Mandir in Bhedaghat, near Jabalpur in Jabalpur district. The third temple at Morena is a beautiful hypaethral temple. The iconographies of the yogini images in the different yogini temples are not uniform. In the Hirapur temple, all yogini images are with their vahanas (vehicles) and in standing posture, with intricate coiffures and distinct sets of jewellery. In the Ranipur Jharial temple the yogini images are in dancing posture. In Bhedaghat temple, yogini images are seated in Lalitasana. (Das, Adyasha: Chausathi Yoginis of Hirapur-from Tantra to Tourism)

The majority of scholars and researchers agree that Tantrism flourished at some point of time between 5th and 6th century. There are ample references to Tantrism in the ancient Vedic literature. In course of time, evidence of the application of tantra in Hinduism, Buddhism and Jainism has also been established. The latter, Buddhism is popularly known as Tantric Buddhism. It flourished between 8th and 12th century A.D.

Odisha is known the world over for the Jagannath

cult which has gained wide popularity. However, this land has been a pot-pourri for multiple sects since aeons. Much before the spread of Jagannath cult in Odisha, the area was known to be a throbbing hub of Shaivaite activities and "prior to that", a stimulating cauldron of tantric and Shakti practices. Distinct marks of Buddhism are also visible in Odisha before it got swayed by tantric practices.

The evolution of the Tantric culture started noticeably in two places in Odisha, one at Hirapur, Khurda and the other at Ranipur Jharial in Balangir. At the time of the advent of Buddhism, Tantrism was highly evolved in Odisha. Buddhist pantheons developed and prospered in Odisha. Gradually the Buddhist tantra gave way to the Hindu tantra. Tara of the Buddhist pantheon became identified as Mangala Nila Saraswati and later as Ramachandi.The Tantric schools of Vajrayana and Tantrayana originated in Odisha and possibly under the influence of the Tantric cults already prevalent in the land. Padmasambhava (Guru Rinpoche), who introduced Vajrayana to Tibet was from Oddiyana which many historians locate in Western Odisha. He was said to be the son of King Indrabhuti.

Though much of Buddhist and Shakti cults consequently lost identity having merged themselves in the evolving religious cults of that time, they have left their imprints on the sands of time in forms of architecture and vague references in religious scriptures. The Yogini cult is one such cult which having found its origin from the Shakti form of worship, prospered well in the 8th century Odisha. The famous 64 yogini temples of Hirapur and Ranipur Jharial are mementos of the significance of this now extinct cult from Odisha. An interesting point is the importance of the worship of the Sacred Feminine with the patronage of the rulers of the state, indicated by the location of both the

Yogini temples in close proximity to the capital. Hirapur is on the outskirts of Bhubaneswar, in and around which capitals were located. Ranipur Jharial was itself the centre of the state and otherwise, in proximity to capitals like Sonpur, Titilagarh and Patnagarh.

Not much is known about the yogini cult and the various tantric practices undertaken by them is still shrouded in mysticism. In fact, so much secrecy was maintained about the practice of this cult, that mere mention of this term would create awe and fear among people. The main reason behind this, probably, is the secrecy of the Yogini cult which is kept in dark from the common mass. Also the images of the yoginis are sculpted with demonic expressions and other dark attributes which evoked fear among the devotees. When the yoginis are depicted in sculpture or described in text, they often have the heads of various birds such as: parrots, hawks, peacocks, eagles, pigeons, and owls.

Apart from this, yoginis are associated with cemeteries and battle-fields where they are said to devour the dead. They were worshipped by kings and soldiers before going on a battle for good luck and victory. Yoginis find mention in the Rudra Upanishad where it is stated that Lord Shiva after slaying Jalandhara summoned the Yoginis (Sapta-matrika) to the battlefield and asked them to devour the flesh of the demon and drink the blood.

Mythology apart, the origin of the Yoginis can be traced back to small, rural villages. They are local village goddesses, grama devatis, who preside over the welfare of an individual village. Through Tantrism, these local deities were able to gain new forms and vitality as a group of goddesses who could impart magical powers to their worshippers.

In the villages of Odisha, the Yoginis are the favoured deities. Each grama devi, be she Ramchandi, Shyamkali, Harachandi, Tarini, Viraja, Bhagavati, Durgamata, Sarala, Bhadrakali, Kamakhya, Bhabani, Mangala etc., presides over the welfare of the village. These village goddesses seem to have been gradually transformed and consolidated into potent numerical groupings of sixty-four (sometimes eighty-one, sometimes forty-two) acquiring thereby a totally different character. It was Tantrism that elevated these local deities and gave them new form and vigour as a group of goddesses who could bestow magical powers with a view to destruction of the enemies.

There are four main traditions that are associated with the cult of the yoginis and how they developed from their tribal beginnings and became integrated into orthodox beliefs. All four of the traditions revolve around the idea that the yoginis were minor divinities to greater goddesses. The first tradition is the idea of the yoginis as aspects of the Devi or Great Goddess. The yoginis were said to be formed from different parts of the Devi, including her voice, sweat, navel, forehead, cheeks, lips, ears, limbs, toe nails, womb, and her anger. In the 11th century collection of myths, the Kathasaritsagara, a yogini is one of a class of females with magical powers, sorceresses sometimes enumerated as 8, 60, 64 or 65. The Hatha Yoga Pradipika also mentions Yoginis. It is a classic fifteenth century Sanskrit manual on ha ha yoga, written by Svatmarama, who connects the teaching's lineage to Matsyendranath of the Nathas.

The second tradition is the idea that the yoginis are attendant deities of the Great Goddess. This tradition is thought to have developed from the earlier tradition of Shiva and his gana attendants. As per tradition, the 64 yoginis were subsidiary deities who served Goddess Kali and the Bhairav form of Shiva and were part of the battles waged by the goddess to restore Dharma. Shrimad Bhagavat Purana also refers to the Yoginis as functionaries of the Goddess. Some of the terms used in Hindu scriptures describe them as Akshobhya, Rakshakarni, Rakshasi, Divyayogi, Siddhayogi and Mahayogi etc. Each Matrika worshipped in Hinduism, especially in Tanrtic cult has her own group of Yoginis as attendants.

The third tradition focuses on the yoginis as acolytes of the Great Goddess: the matrukas. These seven goddesses symbolise the motherly trait and have a logical, esoteric, and conceptual sequence. Sometimes the Sapta Matrikas are portrayed in a deeper philosophical conceptual meaning with the eight divinities involved in the creation of universe in a serial logical order.

- Brahmi or Brahmani representing the unmanifested sound, the creator of the universe.
- Vaishnavi – The one who gives the universe a definite shape.
- Maheshvari - gives individuality to all created beings.
- Kaumari bestows the force of aspirations.
- Varahi - symbolizing the power of assimilation and enjoyment.
- Aindri or Indrani - the immense power that destroys whatever opposes the cosmic law.
- Chamunda - the power of spiritual awakening.

The fourth and final tradition centres on the thought of the yoginis as patrons of the goddess of the Kaulas. The prevalence of Tantric ways led to the association of Yoginis with a specific tantric sect called Kaulas.

The Yoginis are the deification of advanced, adept and astute female practitioners of Yogic and tantric practices.

They are the internalized conception, symbolic personification of the chakras and energy centres inside the human body and being which is a microcosm and a reflection of the cosmos.

Though the leaders of the modern Yoga-asana & meditation tradition have often been male, the vast majority of modern practitioners are female, including many who have attained mastery via steadfast awareness through the Shakti sensations of menses, fertility, childbirth, and breastfeeding. In the Shakta branch of Hinduism, creation myths place the Divine Feminine at their centre, taking the Tantric view that the nature of the Cosmos (or Macrocosm) is reflected in the human body (or Microcosm), and it is the Female who gestates and gives birth to new life. "Only the female can awaken the muladhara chakra (the seat of the Kundalini-shakti) via fertility and sexuality; the male must use Kriya Yoga."

In some branches of Tantra Yoga, ten wisdom goddesses (or dakinis) serve as models for a Yogini's disposition and behaviour. In the mythological context, the word Yogini may indicate an advanced Yoga practitioner who is one or more of the following:

A female who is an associate or attendant of Durga, a fierce aspect of the Divine Feminine, who slays illusion and delusion through insight and liberation.

In several Tantric cults, the term refers to an initiated female who may take part in maithuna tantric rituals. According to the *Hatha-Yoga-Pradipika* text, a yogini is more specifically a woman initiate, who can preserve her own genital ejaculate (rajas) and contain the male semen (bindu) by means of the practice of the vajroli-mudra, also practiced in reverse by advanced yogis.

The Yogini cult has its origin in the simple tribal and

folk tradition of India that, by the 7th-8th centuries A.D., in conjunction with the "Sakta-Tantric" form, meaning the worship of the Mother Goddess combined with certain magical rituals, had acquired a more definite shape. A large body of Tantric texts and a similar number of shrines found in various parts of the country clearly reveal that several inexhaustible attempts made by its exponents and followers went a long way to popularize this esoteric cult between the 9th and 12th century.

Some later inscriptions found in certain Yogini temples further indicate that the cult was practiced even in the 16th century. It is still not clear as to when exactly the Yogini cult bowed out of limelight, and equally intriguing as to why its temples were abandoned. The entire phenomenon of Yogini worship and the construction of temples has its roots outside the folds of orthodox Brahminical tradition. The Yogini in the shape of a Shakta-Tantric cult came into existence in the 7th-8th century AD. It continued to flourish as an important manifestation of Shakta Tantrism. This cult with primitive ideas on the efficacy of magical rituals and spells, sounds and gestures, is a movement that has a deep connection with rural and tribal traditions. If we were to look for the origin of the Yoginis, we must turn to the simple village cults and to the gram devis, the local village goddesses.

The remains of Yogini temples in various parts of the country clearly reveal that the exponents and followers of this esoteric cult made vigorous attempts to popularize it and this cult was of impelling and vital significance from the 9th to the 12th century. Nine Yogini temples discovered so far are distributed in Odisha, Madhya Pradesh, Uttar Pradesh and in Tamil Nadu. Unfortunately, with the ravage of time, only few of the Yogini temples survive today and

Odisha has the distinction of preserving two of these outstanding temples – one at Hirapur, a picturesque village near Bhubaneswar and another at Ranipur-Jharial in Bolangir district.

The Legends

In the ancient scriptures, Yoginis are often depicted as consorts of 'Yogis', and like their male companions practiced 'Yoga' (meditation) to gain mastery over science and acquire magical powers. "Kaula Marga", a tantric form of worship further includes Yoginis of different categories in its "Chakra" (circle) associated with lord Shiva.

The Chakra is alternatively known as "Yogini Chakra", "Kaula Chakra" (the circle of time) or the "Bhairavi Chakra" (the circle of Bhairavi, the female companion of the terrifying form of Shiva known as "Bhairava"). The 'Marga', or path, defines five ways to perform penance to attain liberation and happiness. They are 'Matsya' (fish), 'Mamsa' (meat), 'Mudra' (parched grain), 'Madya' (liquor) and 'Maithuna' (sexual intercourse). A large collection of historical texts mention that to attain 'Siddhi' (spiritual powers), the 'Sadhakas' (the Tantric worshippers) unanimously offered flesh, blood and wine to the Yoginis, a tradition still in practice in several parts of Odisha. Devotees offer all these things to most of the village goddesses on important festive occasions, in times of crisis, and each time these goddesses manifest themselves in dreams or otherwise to the devotees, demanding such sacrifices.

Often, the Sadhakas took recourse to Maithuna to attain the power of the Yoginis. According to the Kaula path, women of lower caste such as the 'Rajaki' (washerwomen), 'Carmakari' (leather worker), 'Vesya' (prostitute), 'Matangi' (an outcaste) and 'Madhumati' (vintner's caste) are the most suitable partners in the ritual of Maithuna. It further suggests that Maithuna practiced along with yoga leads to the most consummate and soul-lifting physical experience.

Witchcraft

A number of ancient texts recount terrifying stories highlighting the sorcery or witchcrafts aspect of the Yoginis. According to these stories, Yoginis could acquire certain magical powers with which they could transform human beings into animals and birds. A few other stories talk of a category of witches referred to as 'Dakinis', known for their ability to fly, besides their appetite for human flesh.

In Odisha, the ancient practice of witchcraft is still practiced. Among the Santals of Mayurbhanj district, the Santali witches often leave behind their husbands in bed in the midst of the night to assemble in a forest. Completely naked, they spend the rest of the night dancing and singing with 'bongas' (spirits or deities) and lions as their partners. At the break of dawn, they return to their beds, back to being what they originally were. The Santals believe that the 'talent' for witchcraft is not innate, but is attained through strict discipline.

Therianthropism

Often, polymorphism identifies yoginis. Therianthrophic forms are common among yoginis, from horses and lions to snakes and birds. Yoginis are thought to take on physical forms of female animals. (Hatley Shaman, What is a yogini?)

Legend of Chandi Purana

The "Chandi Purana", a 15th century A.D. text, written by Sarala Das of Odisha, refers to Yoginis as forms of the 'Devi' or the Supreme Goddess of the 'Saktas', based on the story of the Goddess 'Chandi' or 'Durga' killing 'Mahisasura' or the buffalo-demon and is a clear reflection of the extreme form of Tantrism practiced in coastal Odisha of those times. According to the text, the Goddess Chandi is said to have liberated numerous number of female soldiers known as Yoginis, who were excessively fond of flesh, blood, bone and marrow. To fulfil these desires, the soldiers fought incessantly with the demons till they were killed and could be consumed. The text states that numerous goats, rams and buffaloes were killed every day to propitiate the Goddess Sarala and the Yoginis.

Vajrayana Buddhism

The Vajrayana or the Tantric form of Buddhism, which evolved against the principles of earlier Buddhism preached by the Buddha himself, had laid great emphasis on the theory of emancipation. The preachers of Vajrayana Buddhism redefined 'Nirvana' (liberation) as 'Shunya' (void), 'Vijnana' and 'Mahasukha' (extreme pleasure) that could be achieved by embracing a woman. In this restructured nirvana, women were designated as 'Shakti', and their union with the 'Sadhaka' came to be known as yoga.

Further, Vajrayana Buddhists were empowered to violate laws, kill human beings, and seduce women. They propounded a common slogan - identical actions by which mortals struggling for hundreds of billions of cycles could liberate the 'Yogin' (the Enlightened Man). Khajuraho is one of the ten most predominant seats of Tantra practice. According to the Tantra tradition, there are certain special sites that are charged with spiritual energy, enabling the seeker to reach her goal more readily. Pandit Rajmani Tigunait documents some of these sites, "The spiritual energy of Banaras, for example, is characterized by knowledge...at Ayodhya, by self-sacrifice...at Kamakhya, siddhis (supernatural powers), and at the site of 64 Yoginis (in Khajuraho), the spiritual energy of Khajuraho enables us to experience our body as a living shrine." Georg

Feuerstein in his book, " Tantra: The Path of Ecstasy", identifies the number 64 with Tantric implications, "as meaningful and sacred to Tantra as the number 108 to the Hindu traditions". He further argues that the number corresponds to the 64 Tantras, the 64 Bhairavas (forms of Shiva) and 64 Kalas (aspects of the Supreme Goddess), as mentioned in certain Tantric texts. Pandit Tigunait also observes, "In the Tantric tradition, the 64 yoginis are the presiding deities that guide and govern the entire fabric of life. They not only hold the body and mind together, but also animate them (prana). Awakening these forces is the essence of spiritual accomplishments."

Erotic Motifs

While there exist multiple explanations for the profusion of erotic imagery in Khajuraho, an attempt can be made to bring some of the most plausible ones to the foreground. With the gradual intensification of feudalism in India, local interests and polities strengthened. Regionalism strongly influenced art forms, and eroticism, an integral part of life, got canonized in art. In the essay 'Sexual Imagery on the Phantasmagorical Castles at Khajuraho', published in the International Journal of Tantric Studies (November 1996), Michael Rabe attributes the erotic imagery to protection. Rabe cites a passage from the Zilpa Prakaza (a contemporary text): " the Naribandha (frieze of a woman) is indispensable in architecture. As a house without a wife, as frolic without a woman, so without (the figure of) a woman, the monument will be of inferior quality. A place without love-images is in the opinion of Kaulacaras (Tantric authorities) always a base, forsaken place, a dark abyss." Whether the Chandella dynasty was motivated by Tantra is unknown, but the belief that Tantra was known in the 9th to 12th centuries finds evidence. Rabe pursues that the famed maithuna couplings stand eloquent testimony to the 'left hand' path of Tantra, the Vamamarga—they embody the principle of 'the yoga of bhoga.' The Tantric tradition frequently juxtaposes yoga (disciplined action) and bhoga (pleasure), underlining a complex integration. Taking the argument further, Georg Feuerstein ponders that the Tantriks neither neurotically embrace sensory pleasures (bhoga), nor do they crave for mystical union (yoga). For them, women are Shakti; sex is the love play between Shiva and Shakti, and pleasure is a modification of supreme bliss. Vijnana Bhairava Tantra (a Tantric text) also explains that it is the mind that is the real cause of bondage or liberation. For those pure in mind, everything is pure. For those whose mind is defiled with misconceptions and base emotions, even the pure is polluted.

By 19th century artist from Rajasthan - Dehejia, Vidya (1986). Yogini Cult and Temples: A Tantric Tradition. National Museum, Janpath, New Delhi. page 21, Public Domain, https://commons.wikimedia.org/w/index.php?curid=95671218

Sanskrit Texts as Sources of Yoginis:
- Puranas: Agni Purana, chapter 52; Markandeya Purana, Kalika Purana, Bhagavata Purana, Matsya Purana, Garuda Purana, Skanda Purana, and Devi Bhagavata Purana.
- Maya Dipika, a rare text.
- Pratishtha Lakshana Sara Samuchchaya.
- Chaturvarga Chintamani of Hemadri; thirteenth century.
- Matottara Tantra; thirteenth century

Khechari Yantra

The scared Khechari Yantra, described in the Matottara Tantra, with its 64 petals, is associated with both the 64 Yoginis and 64 Tantric Kriyas. An examination of the ancient Tantric tradition reveals a particular sanctity assigned to the number eight. The eight mother faculties (tatvas) of the manifested universe, the eight directions with four cardinal and four intermediate points (digbandahs), the eight miraculous yogic powers (ashta siddhis), eight "limbs" of Yoga (ashtanga), eight forms of the Divine Mother (ashta matrikas) are just a few examples.

Although the Yogini tradition of early medieval times also produced temples featuring forty-two and eighty-one Yoginis, the bulk of tantric temples have venerated sixty-four yoginis. A representation of the sixty-four Yoginis is found on the ancient Khechari Yantra. Each of its sixty-four petals represent one of these ancient feminine deities of Tantra, the Yoginis.

The sixty-four practical techniques (kriyas) of trance and transformation correspond with the Yogini energies within nature, all of which interact together to produce spiritual growth when the appropriate catalyst is available. Their purpose is to pull souls out of illusion. This is precisely the significance of both the sixty-four hexagrams seen in the Taoist tradition as well as the sixty-four yoginis of the Shakti Tantric tradition. The Tantric literature itself is said to be composed of sixty-four spiritual books, also referred to as Tantras. In this sense, the word tantra conveys the meaning of "canonical manuscripts". The sixty-four sacred texts of Kaula Tantra are enumerated in classical texts such as the Vamakeshvara-tantra.

Similar references in classical literature includes the sixty-four yogic induced paranormal powers (siddhis), the sixty-four divisions of the arts (kalas), and, within the ancient Saiva Siddhanta tradition, the sixty-four saints (nayanars). There are also sixty-four forms of Bhairava, sixty-four tantric mudras, as well as sixty-four siddhas, beyond even the 18 Maha Siddhas, which are more commonly celebrated, and so on. This sacred number is intimately associated with power and life itself. In the Indian classic, Mahabharata, Lord Krishna fired sixty-four arrows and in a separate skirmish, Bhishma's armour was pierced sixty-four times. The Aitereya Brahmana speaks of the sixty-fourth and final step into the heavenly world.

Characteristic Features of the Yoginis:
- Synthesis of tribal beliefs and Vedic as well as Puranic concepts.
- Each Matrika has her own set of yogini attendants. Matrikas are personified forms of powers of gods. They are usually depicted in a group of seven or eight and they are subsidiary deities.
- Some yoginis are indicative of fearsome aspects. They are believed to have magical powers and they have an important place in tantric traditions.
- The worship of Devi Kamakhya has the invocation of sixty-four yoginis in the worship.
- Some yoginis are zoomorphic deities.
- In the concept of yogini, we see the presence of totemism. Totemism is the identification of a tribe with a particular bird or animal. Most totems have their own story where the totem animal or bird has saved the ancestor of that tribe.

The classification of Yoginis can be on the basis of categories of human or superhuman religious players, like:

Goddess – matr/matrka, mahavidya, sakini, dakini

Demigoddess- apsaras, vidyadhari, yaksi/yaksini, Siva's ganas

Ghost-like being/Malevolent female spirits –bhuta, preta, vetala, pisacha, dakini

Female ascetic- sadhvi, sanyasini, gurvi.

Tantric practitioner

(Keul, Istvan: Yogini's in South Asia)

The Yogini Yantra

"Mathematics is the language of the Gods", it has been stated by Dr. Michio Kaku.

God consciousness is manifested through the medium of mathematics and geometry. On a universal scale, there is a direct relationship between mathematics, sound, and form. In tantra, the geometrical form representing sound (mantra) is a yantra. Each variation of pitch and vibration creates a geometric pattern of expression for that frequency. The sacred geometrical form (yantra) and the divinized sound (mantra) are inextricably intertwined to create tantra.

In worshipping the presiding deity of a yantra, we are acknowledging their presence microcosmically, as the soul within ourselves (Jiva), and macrocosmically, as universal nature (Prakriti).

The tantric tradition states that one must become qualified in order to utilize yantras fully, as the knowledge of sacred geometry is a transitional process of revelations that lead to inner union (antar yoga). In 64 yogini yantra the placement of 64 Yoginis is arranged into an Eight petal (Lotus) Yantra where each petal places eight forms of Yogini.

The Yoginis thus have deep connections with modernity in the continued significance of the Goddess concept; it inspires a quest for the goddess within us, urging us from the mundane to the magnificent.The Yoginis symbolize gender asymmetry, women empowerment and represent a cult that connects the ancient and the obscure with the utterly modern in a magical loop.

Annexure 1

7. Devī Purāṇa

1. Vijayā
2. Maṅgalā
3. Rudrā
4. Dhṛti
5. Śāntī
6. Śivā
7. Kṣamā
8. Siddhi
9. Tupti
10. Umā
11. Puṣṭi
12. Śrī
13. Siddhi
14. Rati
15. Diptā
16. Kānti
17. Yaśā
18. Lakṣmī
19. Īśvarī
20. Vṛiddhi
21. Śakti
22. Jayavatī
23. Brāhmī
24. Jayantī
25. Aparājitā
26. Ajitā
27. Mānasī
28. Kheṭā
29. Diti
30. Māyā
31. Mahāmāyā
32. Kriyā
33. Arundhatī
34. Ghaṇṭā
35. Karṇā
36. Sarpabhūṣaṇi-raudrā
37. Kālinī
38. Mayurī
39. Raudrī
40. Mohanī
41. Ratilālasā
42. Vimalā
43. Gaurī
44. Śaraṇyā
45. Kaśikī
46. Mati
47. Durgā
48. Surupā
49. Śivarūpiṇī
50. Ripuhā
51. Ambikā
52. Carcikā
53. Surapūjitā
54. Vaivāsvatī
55. Kaumarī
56. Maheśvārī
57. Vaiṣṇavī
58. Mahālakṣmī
59. Kārtikī
60. Kauśikī
61. Śivadūtī
62. Śivā
63. Cāmuṇḍā
64. Karṇikā

The list of 64 Yoginis as mentioned in Agni Purana

Annexure 2
Skanda Purana, Kasi Khanda
(Yogini with Animal Names)

1	Gajanana	elephant-faced
2	Simhamukhi	lion-faced
3	Grdrasya	vulture-faced
4	Kakatundika	crow-beaked
5	Ustragriva	camel-necked
6	Hayagriva	horse-necked
7	Varahi	boar
8	Sarabhanana	mythical creature, half horse
9	Ulukika	owl-like
10	Sivarava	jackal-voiced
11	Mayuri	peacock
12	Vikatanana	fearsome-faced
13	Astavaktra	eight-faced
14	Kotaraksi	hollow-eyed
15	Kubja	hunch-backed
16	Vikatalocana	fearsome-eyed
17	Suskodari	dried abdomen
18	Lalajjihva	tongue hanging out
19	Svadamstra	canine-toothed
20	Vanaranana	monkey-faced
21	Rksaksi	bear-eyed
22	Kekaraksi	squint-eyed
23	Brhattunda	large-abdomen
24	Surapriya	fond of wine
25	Kapalahasta	skull-cap in hand
26	Raktaksi	blood-eyed
27	Suki	parrot
28	Syeni	hawk
29	Kapotika	dove
30	Pasahasta	noose in hand
31	Dandahasta	club in hand
32	Pracanda	terrible
33	Candahasta	terrible-handed
34	Sisughini	killer of children
35	Papahantri	destroyer of sins
36	Kali	black one
37	Rudhirapayini	drinker of blood
38	Vasadhaya	holder of earth
39	Garbha-bhaksa	eater of foetus
40	Sava-hasta	corpse in hand
41	Antra-malini	garlanded with intestines
42	Sthula-kesi	rough grip on hair
43	Brhatkuksi	large-girdled
44	Sarpasya	snake-faced
45	Pretavahana	one whose vehicle is a preta
46	Dandasukakara	Venomous one
47	Kraunci	heron
48	Mrgasirsa	deer-headed
49	Vrsanana	ox-faced
50	Vyattasya	open-mouthed
51	Dhumanisvasa	inhaler of smoke
52	Vyomaika	the sky
53	Charanordhvaduk	foot at the top
54	Tapani	burning one
55	Sosani-drsti	one with a shrivelling look
56	Kotari	lives in a hole
57	Schulanasika	large-nosed
58	Vidyutprabha	one with the glow of lightening
59	Bakakasya	crane-faced
60	Marjari	cat
61	Kataputana	departed spirit
62	Attahasa	one with a very loud laugh
63	Kamaksi	eyes of love
64	Mrgaksi	eyes of a deer

The Yogini Temples: Past and Present- an overview of Yogini Temples in India

The Yogini shrines of India are sentinels of historical grandeur, mythology, historical and cultural significance. Regarded independently, each of these monuments appears to be a conundrum. Their common circular and at times rectangular plan constitutes a legitimate variant when compared to other Hindu temple architecture. A deeper appreciation of the temples however, indicates considerable diversity among them. The list of the sixty-four yoginis at the different temples do not correspond to each other, neither to any recognized Puranic list of Yoginis. The temples are as follows :-
Extant: Hirapur, Ranipur-Jharial (Odisha)
Bhedaghat, Khajuraho, Mitaoli/Morena, Badoh, Dudahi (M.P)
Lost: Lokhar, Sahadol, Hinjalgarh, Nareshwar (MP)
     Varanasi, Rikhiyan (UP)
     Mehrauli(Delhi)
     Kaveripakkam(TN)

Chausathi Yogini temple, Hirapur
Bhubaneswar, Odisha

"We are light and dark, sun and moon, male and female, yin and yang; life is composed of opposites, in a continuing cycle of change.... When you are in the light, don't step back into the darkness. Live in that light, and breathe it in fully."

The Yogini Temple at Hirapur, also known as the "Mahamaya Temple", has an ambience that is quite vibrant. The temple conveys an impression of the overwhelming power of its sixty-four Yoginis. Mahamaya, the presiding deity of the temple is found adorned with red cloth and vermilion. The deity continues to be worshipped by the local villagers even today.

The Hirapur Temple, quaint and delicate, is the smallest of the Yogini temples in India. It measures only thirty feet in diameter, and is hardly eight feet high. The temple is built of coarse sandstone blocks with laterite as its foundation. The Yoginis are carved out of fine-grained gray chlorite. The inner walls of the temples have sixty-four niches with Yoginis in place. The small central pavilion has eight niches. Three of these have the images of the remaining of the sixty-four Yoginis, (one statue is missing) while the other four have images of the Bhairavas depicted with erect phalluses as is customary of the images of Shiva in Odisha. The images are about two feet tall, and the niches, in which they are placed, were probably treated as miniature shrines.

The construction of the Yogini temple of Hirapur was initiated by the Bhauma and Somavamsi rulers of Odisha who were known for their tolerance, liberal philosophy and eclecticism. Their rule, which lasted from mid-8th to mid-10th century A.D., has been depicted as the 'Golden Age' mainly due to their contributions in the fields of philosophy and literature. During this period, there was a gradual amalgamation of Shaivism (worship of Shiva), Shaktism (worship of the Mother Goddess) and the Vajrayana, or Tantric form of Mahayana Buddhism in the region. It is believed that the Yogini Temple at Hirapur was built towards the end of the Bhauma rule, in the 9th century A.D. The circular structure of the temple indicates harmony, unity and camaraderie, lack of hierarchy and a sign of completeness; its hypaethral form indicates the sky itself as the ceiling connoting a connection with the infinite .A taller Shiva temple in the centre with slightly smaller circle of Yogini temples together evoke the similarity with a Shiva lingam which is the symbol of the central deity and of the Infinity which Shiva symbolizes.

The sculptures of Hirapur temple are extraordinarily beautiful. Faces are delicately carved often with a gentle smile and with coiffures of various styles and heavily ornamented. The architecture of this temple combines a highly original sculptural tradition with extraordinary craftsmanship. A visit to the Yogini temple at Hirapur marks only the beginning of the journey into Odisha's mysterious past. It also throws light on the role the worship of feminine cults played in promoting harmony through the synthesis of major religious traditions of medieval Odisha.

In this temple, every male deity except Shiva are replaced by a female counterpart including Ganesha. The Yogini Cult, Tantric in nature and tantra itself, projecting the efficacy of magical rituals and spell, sounds and gestures, is intertwined deeply with rural and tribal traditions. There is a diverse range of attitudes toward the tantric traditions, ranging from viewing it as a path to liberation to the relatively widespread associations of the tantric traditions with sorcery and libertine sexuality. In Hinduism, the tantra tradition is most often associated with its goddess tradition called Shaktism, followed by Shaivism and Vaishnavism.

The Yoginis were believed to impart magical powers to their worshippers.
These powers included:
> *anima* (the ability to become very small),
> *laghima* (the power to levitate and to be able to leave your body at will),
> *garima* (the power to become very heavy),
> *mahima* (the power to become large in size),
> *istiva* (the power to control the body and mind of oneself and others),

parakamya (the power to make others do your biding),
vasitva (the power to control the five elements) and kamavasayitva (the power to be able to fulfill all your desires)

(Das, Adyasha, *The Chausathi Yoginis of Hirapur: from Tantra to Tourism*, Black Eagles Books, USA, 2018).

The Yoginis of Hirapur are ornately adorned, have captivating appearances, both terrifying and mesmerizing, and offer life-enhancing energies that bring about fertility, growth, longevity, abundance, material and spiritual well-being. Yoginis are wrathful and sensual, ferocious and seductive, furious and graceful. They hold various tools and weapons, symbolic of what the practitioner needs on his path—a knife to sever attachments, a goad to nudge us along when we are stuck, a bell to clear negativity, a spear for penetrating insight, a bow and arrow for focus, etc. Their mounts are animals, vegetation, and different potent symbols such as a pot, flames, corpse, or drum that lend their powers and mythological significance to the Yoginis.

Chausath Yogini Temple, Khajuraho

The construction of the Chausath Yogini temple located at Khajuraho can be dated to approximately 885 CE. It is the earliest extant temple at the Chandela capital, Khajuraho. The temple has been classified as a monument of national importance by the Archaeological Survey of India. In the Khajuraho temple complex, away from the main group of twenty-three sculpted temples, built in elegant Nagara style of architecture, there is a unique open-air rectangular sanctuary, dedicated to the Chausatha or Sixty-four Yoginis. The Sixty-four Yoginis shrine of

Khajuraho is an important sanctuary of the Yogini cult that was widespread in the vast region between central India and Odisha in the period circa 900 to 1400 and even later. Three large statues of goddesses, found among the ruins, are now located at the Khajuraho museum. The goddesses have been identified as Brahmani, Maheshvari, and Hingalaja or Mahishamardini. These statues are among the oldest sculptures of Khajuraho. The Durga image of the central cell of the Khajuraho Yogini sanctuary is inscribed with the label "Hinghalaja". This name brings to mind the famous pitha Hingula where the head or crown (brahmarandhra) of Sati fell, according to the Sakta texts.

Chausathi Yogini Temple, Morena
Also known as Ekattarso Mahadeva Temple
Mitaoli village Morena

Also known as Ekattarso Mahadeva Temple, this Yogini temple is an 11th-century temple located in Morena district in the state of Madhya Pradesh. It is one of the few well-preserved Yogini temples in the country. The temple is formed by a circular wall with 64 chambers and an open

mandapa in the centre, separated by a courtyard which is circular in shape, where Shiva is deified. This temple is situated on top of a small hill, and is designed on a circular plan. Constructed on a high plinth, it has pillared cloisters that run around the wall facing an open courtyard. The small cells that form 64 subsidiary shrines have a mandapa in front while a circular main shrine stands in the middle of the courtyard. The cells and the main shrine are flat topped, but it is believed that initially each had a shikhara on top. The 64 Yoginis originally placed in the 64 subsidiary shrines are now missing, a Shiva linga has taken their places in each cell. The central shrine also holds a Shivalinga. According to an inscription, the temple was constructed by Maharaja Devapala of the Kacchapagata dynasty, dated VS 1380 (1323 CE).

Chausathi Yogini Temple, Bhedaghat
Madhya Pradesh

The Chausath Yogini Temple nestling on a hill top close to the famous Dhundhar Falls in Bhedaghat, near Jabalpur, is the largest Yogini Temple in India. It consists of a circular structure, with an inner diameter of 116 feet and an outer diameter of 131 feet. The temple symbolizes the glory of the Kalchuri dynasty. Constructed in the 10th century during the pinnacle of the Kalchuri Kingdom it has a noticeable structural resemblance to the temples of Khajuraho. Constructed with local granite, it is the abode of Goddess Durga along with 64 yoginis. The main shrine has idols of Lord Shiva and his consort Goddess Parvati riding on Nandi. The design of the temple is simple but the idols of yoginis depict unique postures and exquisite carving. The cloister consists of 84 square pillars with 81 cells and 3 entrances, two on west and one on south-east. Despite the existence of 81 niches for the yoginis, researchers and scholars refer to it as the Chausath Yogini temple. As indicated by the Sri Matottara Tantra, the eighty-one Yogini temple could have been a royal temple.

Chausathi Yogini Temple
Chousati Ghat, Varanasi

The Kashi Khanda described the ghat and images of Yoginis, and mentioned the two Jala-Tirthas ("water associated sacred spots"). This ghat had privilege to provide shelter to a great Sanskrit scholar Madhusudan Sarasvati (CE 1540-1623). Till 18th century the main image of the Chausathi Devi was in the Rana Mahal, a palace nearby, and was later shifted to its present site.

Chousati (Chausathi) Ghat is located south of Dasaswamedh Ghat next to Digpatiya Ghat. It is named after 64 (chausatha) goddesses. The steep steps lead to the Chausath Yogini Temple. With my deep interest in the Yogini cult, how could I not visit this temple? With the help of the boatman-guide and colleagues, few of us dared the climb up the steep steps. The narrow alleys housed small, quaint hotels on both sides, with a terrific view of the ghats and the Ganges. The temple is not hypaethral and has a ceiling now. The Mahut and his family stay on the floor above. The sixty-four Yogini statues are also missing. Goddess Kali rules resplendent. Many Hindus come to the temple during the new moon day of the month of Chaitra, an auspicious day when they take a dip in the Ganga.

Yogmaya Temple
Mehrauli, Delhi

A Hindu temple, it is a Shakti peetha dedicated to the sister of Krishna, and situated close to the Qutb complex earlier known as Yoginipura. According to local priests this is one of 27 temples destroyed by Mahmud Ghazni and later by Mamluks. It is the only surviving temple belonging to the pre-sultanate period. Hindu king Samrat Vikramaditya Hemu reconstructed the temple and restored it from ruins.

Forty- two Yogini shrines

Dudahi

The temple at Dudahi, locally famous as Akhada, near Lalitpur in Uttar Pradesh, is now in ruins and its legacy is considered lost. The temple had a circular plan with niches for 42 yoginis. The circle measures 50 feet in diameter.

Badoh
Gadarmal Devi temple, Badoh, Uttar Pradesh

At a short distance from Dudahi, at Badoh in Vidisha district, Madhya Pradesh, the Gadarmal Devi temple is located. This is yet another 42-niche yogini temple and is rectangular in design. Eighteen damaged images of the goddesses that were originally placed in the niches of the temple are preserved from the waist down. It is composed of a rectangular shrine and a tall and massive Shikhara. According to Vidya Dehejia, the yogini temple must once have been hypaethral. It is believed that the temple was built by herdsmen and was popularly called Gadarmal Devi Temple among locals. It is similar to Teli-Ka Mandir in Gwalior fort in its combination of two architectural styles, Pratihara and Parmara. The temple is surrounded by 7 ruined shrines. (C.9th CAD). (*"Gadarmal Temple", Archaeological Survey of India. Retrieved 11 December 2018.*)

Source: G.S.Sekhawat

Lost, ancient Yogini Temples

Several yogini temples have been lost over time, whether through planned destruction or looting. These include the following temples:

Lokhari

The ruins of an ancient 10th century yogini temple is found to exist on a hilltop at Lokhari, Banda District, Uttar Pradesh. Lokhari is a small, anonymous village in the Mau subdivision of Banda district, Bundelkhand region of Uttar Pradesh. The ancient temple at Lokhari was identified as a historically significant site after the discovery of yogini sculptures. The site confirms the lost tradition of esoteric forms of worship prevalent in that region in the tenth century CE.

A group of twenty images, most of them theriomorphic, the figures having the heads of animals such as horse, cow, rabbit, snake, buffalo, goat, bear, and deer, has been recorded. Dr. Vidya Dehejia describes these as striking rather than artistic. During her visit to the site several years ago, she had seen and written about these statues.

Yogini Vrishanana, Pratihara Dynasty, from Lokhari, Uttar Pradesh, Stone, 10th century C.E., National Museum, New Delhi, India.

Vrishanana Yogini sits on an unornamented stone slab in 'lalitasana', holding a club in the left hand and a 'bilva' fruit in the right. Her 'vahana' is a swan that's pecking the bilva. The Yogini has a chiselled body with full breasts. Her eyes are meditative, half-closed in contemplation and the buffalo face is serene and meditative.

She is adorned with a necklace, anklets, bangles and a girdle on the waist — similar to the jewellery of tribal communities.

Naresar

Another set of twenty 10th century images, with careless later inscriptions from the 12th century, was rescued from Nareshwar (also called Naleshvar and Naresar) in Madhya Pradesh, a site which still has some twenty small Shaivite temples, to the Gwalior Museum situated not far away. The site of Naresar, near Gwalior, Madhya Pradesh is noteworthy for a unique yoni sculpture which houses 15 smaller yonis within itself. The archaeological survey of India is trying to restore the ancient temple complex at Naresar to its former glory when it existed as a secluded spot of meditative worship.

Hinglajgarh

Hinglajgarh is named after the goddess Hinglaj Devi, the *kuldevi* of Kshatriyas & Brahamkshtriya. Hinglaj is an important Hindu pilgrimage destination in Balochistan, Pakistan. The Kshatriyas, in ancient times travelled between Baluchistan and India.

The site of Hinglajgarh, situated on the border of Madhya Pradesh and Rajasthan, was cleared for the building of the Gandhi Sagar Dam. In the process, several sculptural remains and ruined statues were found. The rescued statues contain substantial fragments of yogini images to indicate the presence of a Yogini temple at this site once. Dehejia corroborates this too. Most of the statues are now found in museums at Bhopal, Indore and Jhansi.

The Yoginis of Hinjalgarh are all seated. A halo with carved petals frames the head of each Yogini. The statues are beautifully styled and appear to be contemporary with the yoginis found at Naresar. Yogini Indrani, Chamunda and Vainayaki are clearly discernible.

Tantrism has been inculcated as an intrinsic component of the worship of the Divine Mother; so the sculptors and artisans of Hinglajgarh created exquisite masterpieces of Divine Mother as a *Yogini*. The sculptures of Divine Mother as *Katyayani, Vinayaki, Aparajitha, Bhuvaneshwari* and *Bagalamukhi* and others have been found here. It is evident from the discovery of hundreds of sculptures and idols of unparalleled craftsmanship that Hinglajgarh at one time occupied a seat of prominence in arts and sculpture. (www.sahasa.in)

Mahishamardhani Durga slaying Mahisha, at Indore Central Museum; Period : 900-999 CE; from Hinglajgarh, Mandsaur, MP; Material : Greyish Pale Stone; Dimensions : 38 x 33 cm. Obviously in her attempt to slay the Asura, she is shown holding its head firmly in one hand and Image Courtesy VMIS, Ravichandran KP

A mutilated Mahishamardhani in its lower part, exhibited at Indore Central Museum; Period : 900-999 CE; From Hinglajgarh, Mandsaur, MP; Image Courtesy VMIS, Ravichandran KP

Mahishamardhani Durga slaying Mahishasura; From Indore Central Museum; Period: 900-999 CE; From Hinglajgarh, Mandsaur, MP; Material: Dark Grey Sandstone; Dimensions: 92 x 67 cm. Obviously eight armed or more with no attributed identifiable in Her mutilated state, Her Trident pierces the body of the Buffalo while Her Chakra is seen embedded on the body. Look at the fallen Asura below !!! Image Courtesy VMIS, Ravichandran KP

Rikhiyan

Situated close to Khajuraho, in the Banda District, Uttar Pradesh, are the ruins of a rectangular 64-Yogini temple in the Rikhiyan valley. The site was identified in 1909 when ten slabs containing carvings of four yoginis in each were found. Dehejia states that the multiples of 4 suggest a 64-Yogini total, while the straightness of the slabs implies a rectangular plan (as at Khajuraho). The slabs depict the Yoginis on a completely plain background without the attendant figures found normally. They sit in the ceremonial pose of Lalitasana, one leg resting on their vahana. They have "heavy breasts, broad waist[s] and large stomach[s]". One has the head of a horse, and holds a corpse, a severed head, a club, and a bell, and so may be Hayanana, "The Horse-headed". This and other Yoginis shown with corpses link the temple to a corpse ritual. Also photographed in 1909 were three three-Matrika slabs; Dehejia suggests that these formed part of a rectangular shrine to the Eight Matrikas accompanied by Ganesh.(Dehejia, Yogini Cult and Temples)

Shahdol

Yogini images found in the Shahdol district (ancient texts refer to it as Sahasa-dollaka) in Madhya Pradesh are now preserved at Dhubela Museum near Khajuraho, the Indian Museum at Calcutta, and the village temples of Antara and Panchgaon in Shahdol district. The yoginis are seated in the ceremonial Lalitasana pose, and they have haloes along with flying figures around their heads. Dehejia states that the statues could have belonged to two Yogini temples as there are some seated and some others standing. However, all the statues have been carved from the same variety of sandstone.

Animal headed Yoginis from Shahdol the horse headed is at Dhubela Museum and the others are at the Museum in Kolkata(Calcutta)
Source: Stella Dupuis

Kanchipuram or Kaveripakkam

Dehejia has discussed about yogini images of the Chola period, around 900 AD, recovered from northern Tamil Nadu. These include one now in the British Museum, others in the Madras Museum, the Brooklyn Museum, the Minneapolis Institute of Arts, the Detroit Institute of Art, and the Royal Ontario Museum. The British Museum yogini is ascribed to Kanchipuram; many sculptures of the same style were recovered from a large "tank" (artificial lake) at Kaveripakkam, seemingly derived from nearby temples. The image formed part of a large set of yoginis.

Source: Stella Dupuis
Kanchipuram yoginis now in Paris, London, Zurich, Toronto, Detroit, Washington, Minneapolis & Chennai.

West Bengal

There is evidence from inscriptions and archaeology that several yogini temples were built in Bengal. Dehejia notes that "texts on the Kaula Chakrapuja [worship in the tantric circle] indirectly reveal their Bengali origin in specifying varieties of fish known only in Bengal waters" and that "most of the texts containing lists of Yoginis were written in Bengal".

RANIPUR JHARIAL
The Abode of the Chausathi Yoginis

"I have created all worlds at my will, without being urged by any higher being, and I dwell within them. I permeate the earth and heaven, all created entities with my greatness, and dwell in them as eternal and in?nite consciousness."
Devi Sukta, Rigveda 10.125.8, Translated by June McDaniel.

The Chausathi Yogini Temple of Ranipur Jharial, Balangir District, Odisha, is one of the two hypaethral temples of Odisha celebrating the mystic, elusive yoginis. The presence of other temples around it is an indicator that it was a significant site since ancient times. Ranipur Jharial Yogini temples were highlighted by the writings of by Major-General John Campbell in 1853.

"The 120 temples, the circular temple or enclosure and the brick temple reported by Col.Campbell certainly mean the stone temples, the Chausath Yogini temple and the Indralath brick temple at Ranipur Jharial in the present Balangir district. This discovery of Major General Campbell is the earliest of it's kind, as it occurred in 1853. (Panda, Sasanka S. (December 2005). "Archaeological Explorations and Excavations in Western Orissa". Orissa Review. Retrieved 26 October 2020.)

The villages of Ranipur Jharial have noticeable traces of their ancient heritage. Also referred to as 'Soma Tirtha' in scriptures, the archaeological site dates back to the 9th/10th century AD, pertaining to the reign of the Somavanshi Keshari kings. Shaivism, Vaishnavism, Buddhism and Tantrism, in a unique amalgamation that greatly influenced the region. The hypaethral Yogini temple provides a glimpse into the religious and occult practices of medieval times that are still alive in Odisha's tribal traditions and folklore. The river Tong or Tong Jor, a tributary of Tel flows nearby.

The Tel valley is archaeologically very rich and Ranipur Jharial occupies a central position surrounded by a chain of historical sites like Nrusinghnath, Maraguda, Podagarh, Asurgarh, Belkhandi, Saintala and Patnagarh all around. At present the archaeological complex is found spread on a vast flat rocky surface.

In the epigraph inscribed on the lintel of the Someswar temple, the site has been described as Soma Tirtha, which finds mention in the Puranas dating back to 3rd/4th century A.D. It is thus evident that since 3rd/4th century Ranipur-Jharial had been celebrated as a Shaiva Tirtha. Shaivism had been popular in ancient Kosala and Kantara region since the days of the Nalas who ruled over this region from the middle of the fourth century A.D. as aptly described by C.B. Patel.

This is corroborated by the excavation at Maraguda in Nawapara district where a Shaiva Vihar of circa 4th/5th century A.D. has been excavated. The destruction of the Maraguda Shaiva Vihar led the Shaivacharyas to proceed in the north westernly direction and subsequently they

founded the Shaiva establishment at the ancient Somatirtha referred to in the Puranas. The kernel of Tantricism that originated at Maraguda had fuller efflorescence at Ranipur-Jharial. The Tantric Vajrayana and Sahajayana which Indrabhuti and Laxmikara of ancient Sambala (modern Sambalpur) propounded, were popularized in this region. However, Ranipur-Jharial witnessed great religious development during the reign of the Somavansis who ruled over this tract in 8th/9th century A.D. Most of the existing monuments can be assigned to this period. When exactly this place was deserted is difficult to say due to want of evidence. The Muslim invasion in the 15th century might be a factor for its downfall. We believe systematic exploration and excavations in this locality will throw new light on the history and culture of this place. From surface observation, it appears that the site might have still greater remote antiquity. We noticed here foot print emblem, reminiscent of early Buddhist worship of anoconic diction. Thus prior to 3rd century A.D. probably Ranipur-Jharial had Buddhist association. (Patel, Dr. C.B, Monumental Efflorescence of Ranipur Jharial).

The Chausathi Yogini temple at Ranipur Jharial is situated on the top of a hill in seclusion from the village settlements located nearby. The Yogini temple shares remarkable topographical similarities with other Yogini sites like the one at Mitaoli and Bhedaghat at Madhya Pradesh. The rugged landscape and the presence of a water body nearby probably created an ideal setting for female mendicants to meditate and practice austerities. The circular hypaethral form of the Yogini temples is an important architectural feature for it allows the circulation of divine cosmic energy that is an integral part of these sites. This idea of the "circulation of divine energy" is a fundamental premise of Sufism with the circular dance of whirling dervishes as well as in shamanic practices. At the site, we also see the ancient remains of a once existing "maze" –a series of concentric circles –a concept, which is shared by numerous belief systems in Sufism, Christianity and Buddhism. This "maze" allows entry for two people and is not just a physical encounter but also a spiritual union with the Higher Form. A maze is an ancient symbol representing

wholeness, combining the imagery of the circle and the spiral into a meandering but path directed by purpose. It represents a journey to our own centre and back again out into the world, establishing a connection between the internal and external. Mazes have been used as meditation and prayer tools since ancient times. They have been found in ancient Crete, Egypt, and Etruscia; they have been inscribed on Neolithic tombs. The maze has always been associated with unity with God and conversation with the divine, with spirituality, worship, and the sacred mystery.

The central shrine contains an image of dancing Shiva; all the Yogini images are, similarly shown dancing. Here an eight handed figure of Lord Siva is seen to be dancing in Ananda Tandava on a platform of the height of around two feet. It is a roofed platform and of the height of around seven feet. The image of the Lord is nearly four feet in height. A snake is going around his waist-portion. It creeps up and peeps above his left shoulder. A Jatamukuta is adorning his head and Makara Kundalas are hanging from his ears. He is Urdhvalinga (Penis Erectus). In both of his upper hands, which are raised above his head, he is holding a long snake. The objects in his middle upper and lower right hands are Trisula (small trident) and Dambaru respectively, the Dambaru being placed on his right thigh. In his middle upper and lower left hands are Gada and Aksamala respectively. The lowest left hand is completely broken. His proper right hand is just above the naval in the Gajahasta pose. His left leg is on the back of his Vahana the Nandi bull, whose profiled figure is carved on the pedestal. The right leg is resting upon the toe on the left shoulder of a fourhanded Ganesa, who is dancing below in the same Ananda Tandava posture. In the left lower hand of Ganesa is a Laddupatra, from which he is picking up laddu by extending his proboscis. His lower right hand is in the same Gajahasta pose like that of Siva and in his upper right hand is a Parasu.

The Nataraja images of Mahagaon, Dungripali (Budhikomna) Deogaon (Banei), Sarsara (Banei), Bad Jagannath temple (Sonepur) and Ranipur Jharial (both of the Chausath Yogini Pitha and the Indralath brick temple) are Urdhvalinga. Images with Urdhvalinga have been found as early as the Kushana period. Such images are generally found in Assam, Bengal and Orissa. This feature of Urdhva-Retas is defined as the indication of the state of perpetual celibacy (Govindarajan, Hema; The Nataraja Image from Asanpat, article published in Dimensions of Indian ArtPupul Jayakar Seventy', Vol.I, ed. by Lokesh Chandra and Yotindra Nath, Agam Kala Prakashan, Delhi, 1986, p.145.)

This procedure of open-air worship of Nataraja along with the Matrkas and Yoginis is suggestive of these Pithas possibly used by the Kapalikas for sexo-yogic practices. Learned scholar Dr. H.C. Das has rightly put that "the hypaethral 64 Yogini temple is the expression of intense

form of Tantricism, where Nataraja, the central figure is encircled by terrifying images of 64 Yoginis. (Rao, T.A. Gopinatha, Elements of Hindu Iconography, Vol.II, Part-I, Indological Book House, Varanasi, 1971 (Second Edition), pp.223-231 ff.)

The niches arranged around the central shrine contain the Yogini images. Beglar visited this place in 1874-75 and has also noted them in his writings. The niches measure 100 x 50 cm.

Collectives or groupings of female deities have a long-standing place in history, mythology, legend and the natural landscape. Hence Chausathi Yoginis are the sacred female goddesses wherein they are 64 and 81 yoginis in numbers. Chausathi Yogini Temple of Ranipur Jharial (Odisha) is a comparatively less visited site despite being listed as one of the centrally protected monuments. A great array of heritage products is found in the temple complex, which definitely requires more attention. Lack of awareness of the immense religious significance of the site has turned it into a destination for leisure, with activities endangering the character of the place. The valuable objects and the unique aspects of the temple like iconography, the sacred yogini cult, and sacred geometry embedded in the cultural tradition and belief system should be treasured.

At Ranipur Jharial, a three-headed and eight-handed figure of Bhairava in the dancing pose of Ananda Tandava is enshrined in an open Mandapa in the centre of the circular open air temple, where the sixty-four Yoginis are placed in the dancing posture of Adbhu. Although this image of Ranipur Jharial has been taken as the Nataraja aspect of Lord Siva by scholars, this researcher disagrees and thinks it to be "Urdhvalinga Bhairava" the central deity of the Chausath Yoginipitha. The Lord's left foot is placed on the back of the crouching bull Nandi, who is looking up at the Lord with raised head. Near the right foot of the dancing Bhairava of Ranipur Jharial, there is a four-handed seated figure of Ganesha. The dancing Bhairava is adorned with a broad necklace, armlets, Jatamukuta and Sankha-Patra Kundalas. A Sarpa is encircling his waist and raising its hood above his left shoulder. He is also holding another snake over his head in his upper hands. They are the famous snakes, Taksaka and Dhananjaya, who helped Lord Shiva during his fight with Andhakasura. The Lord is holding a small trident (Sula) in his upper left hand and a Dambaru placed on his right thigh which he holds in his third right hand. His fourth right hand is below his chest portion in Varadamudra. Similarly, in his upper left hand, he is holding a club (Gada) and in the third left hand a rosary (Aksamala) respectively. His eyes are closed. It seems to be the pacified form of the Lord. Siva in his Ugra aspect of Bhairava was a Yogi, who troubled the Yoginis.

A story in Kathasaritasagara mentions that once, at midnight Chandrasvamin saw a circle of Matrkas (Matruchakra), headed by Narayani (Vaishnavi), who were impatiently waiting for Bhairava to present him with various gifts. (Orissa Review * January - 2004). Immediately after goddess Narayani finished her narration explaining the delay of Lord Bhairava, the Lord of the Circle of Mothers arrived there. The Matrkas there-after presented their gifts to him, after which he danced and sported with the Yoginis. (Sarasvath, K.S.; Kathasaritasagara, Patna, 1961, Ch.6, Vs. 76-106; C.H. Tawney, The Kathasaritasagara, London, 1880, p.552.)

(Tandavena Ksanam Nrtyannakridad Yoginisahah).

In the Agni Purana, we find the mention of Bhairava as the Lord of the Mothers (Matrunatha), who is to be worshipped at the centre of the mothers (Matrumadhye Pujyah). In the Tantrika Kaula texts like Kularnava and Meru Tantra, Bhairava has been mentioned as the central deity, whose position is to be at the centre of the Circle of Yoginis (Yoginichakramadhyastham). (Kularnava, Ch.8, V.32. Also Meru Tantra in Sham Sher Dhana's book Brhat Purascaryarnava, 4 Vols., Kathmandu, Vol.III, p.426.

The Yoginis of Ranipur Jharial: Rare Features
- At least fifteen Yogini images are found holding the trident.
- Yoginis No 1 and No 12 have three faces and hold a trident.
- Many Yoginis found at Hirapur are not found at Ranipur Jharial.
- There is no sign of skeletal Chamunda or sow-faced Varahi, nor of Vaisnavi, Aindri or Kaumari. It seems that at Ranipur Jharial, as at Hirapur, we see a tradition that differentiated between the Matrkas and Yoginis (Dehejia, Vidya. Yogini Cult and Temples- a Tantric Tradition).
- Made of coarse sandstone, most of the images have not withstood the wear and tear of time. The Vahanas of most Yoginis have been completely defaced except four images.
- Fourteen Yogini images have distinct animal heads, numbering more than such images at Hirapur Chausathi Yogini temple.

Apart from the fact that many of the statues are damaged beyond recognition, many Yogini statues are missing. Several studies and research draw comparisons between the two Yogini temples of Odisha, at Hirapur and Ranipur Jharial respectively. While the statues at Hirapur are fine sculptures with chiseled features, exquisite to the last detail, the Ranipur Jharial Yoginis are comparatively plain. The reason is that an inferior variety of sandstone has been used at Ranipur Jharial, which has been eroded over time. The deterioration of some of the finest statues of antiquity and other valuable pieces of sculpture of this shrine can be attributed to the choice of stone.

Odissi Dance and the Chausathi Yoginis

"Dance, an integral component of our cultural heritage, is the narration of a magical story, that recites on lips, illuminate's imaginations and embraces the most sacred depths of souls. It is the timeless interpretation of life".

Odisha is the home of Odissi, one of the widely practiced Indian, classical dance forms. Sensuous and sublime, Odissi is a dance that is an intermingling of love and passion, divine and the human. The *Natya Shastra* mentions many regional varieties, like the Odra Magadha etc. which could have been the earliest initial forms of present day Odissi.

Archaeological evidence of this dance form dating

back to the 2nd century B.C. is found in the caves of Udayagiri and Khandagiri near Bhubaneshwar. Later, innumerable examples of the Buddhist sculptures, the tantric images of dancing Yoginis, the Nataraja, and other celestial musicians and dancers of early Shaivite temples bear testimony to a continuing tradition of dance from the 2nd century B.C.E to the 10th century C.E. These influences found synthesis in a unique philosophy- the **dharma** or **faith** of Jagannath. With Hinduism taking roots in Odisha by about the 7th century A.D., many imposing temples were erected. The magnificent Sun Temple at Konarak, built in the 13th century, with its **Natya mandap** or Hall of dance, marks the culmination of the temple building activity in Odisha. (Centre for Cultural Resources and Training)

The ancient heritage of Odissi is found in several ancient sites and monuments of Odisha: the dance scene relief from the Rani Gumpha Caves, the largest cave among the caves of Udayagiri and Khandagiri to the beautiful alasakanyas of Rajarani and Mukteshwar temples and the assertive yoginis of Hirapur and Ranipur Jharial. Guru Surendranath Jena who did not always conform to the established canons of Odissi was very deeply influenced by the Chausathi Yoginis of Hirapur. "Shakti Rupa Yogini", a solo performance choreographed by him, was a homage to the Hirapur Yoginis. (Royo, Lopez Alessandra," Guru Surendranath Jena: Subverting the Reconstituted Odissi Canon, Dance Matters)

Dance in Odisha has had a flourishing existence since second century B.C. due to the political and artistic patronage by several kings belonging to multiple dynasties with multiple religious' affiliations (Maitra 165). It has been influenced by Shakta Tantrism (worshipping goddess

Sakti), Vaishnavism (worshipping male deity Visnu), and Saivism (worshipping Siva) within Hinduism as well as other religions, namely, Buddhism, Islam, and Jainism. Several important dynasties, the Chedi, the Bhauma-Kara, the Somavamsi-Kesari, the Ganga, the Surya, and the Mughals ruled Odisha from the pre-Christian era until the nineteenth century C.E. The temples in Odisha evidence the widespread popularity of dance over the centuries. In the post-Kharavela period, the Bhauma-Karas ruled over Odisha until the eighth century C.E. during which Buddhism and Tantrism were influential and received royal patronage. Buddhist goddesses such as Heruka, Marichi, Vajravarahi, Achala, and Aparajita, feature in the dance sculptures of Udayagiri, Lalitgiri, Ratnagiri, and Alatagiri. Charles Louis Fabri, a Hungarian Indologist and art critic, mentions the dancing image in the monastery of Ratnagiri dating back to 850 C.E. The Chausathi Jogini Temple at Hirapur, a Tantric temple constructed in the ninth century C.E. by queen Hiradevi of the Bramha dynasty, has numerous dancing postures of Bhairav, Tantric god and Yogini, Tantric goddess.

With the receding influence of Jainism and Buddhism, Shaivite (worshipping Hindu male god Siva) and Shakta (worshipping Hindu female goddess Sakti) cults started emerging with the successive occupation of parts of Odisha by the Somavamsi-Kesaris. Earlier, Bhauma-Karas had merged indigenous forms of worship with Shakti doctrine celebrating the goddess in her grotesque beauty. The Somavamsi-Kesaris embraced Shaivism, worshipping of Siva, while integrating Buddhist and Jain influences in their rituals. They replaced the frightful images with benign and softened depictions of the goddess, in what dance-scholar Banerji sums up "as an abrupt movement from bhayanak and bibhatsa to shringar and shanti" (Odissi Dance 164).

In practice, by the tenth century, Tantra was a ritual and philosophical system that harnessed the divine energy within the human body considered to be the microcosm of the spiritual universe. Earlier in this section, I noted that Tantrism was practiced in Odisha since the eighth century. In fact, Tantrism and Shaktism (worshipping the goddess Sakti) merged as the Shakta Tantra that ritually harnessed and channeled the eternal feminine principle, or Sakti, for spiritual liberation. In her ethnographic encounter with the Maharis in Odisha, Anthropologist Frédérique Apffel-Marglin defines Sakti as a "female power, engendering both life and death in its temporal unfolding". Unlike Vaisnavite religious practices that required high caste Brahmanical priests to perform ritual services,16 Shakta Tantra rituals were performed by Tantrics or ritual worshippers of Sakti (the eternal female principle) who deliberately broke the orthodox injunctions posed by the Brahmanical system. In the Jagannath temple, Mahari dance infused Shakta Tantric (goddess worship) into the Vaishnavite fold (the worship of Hindu male god Visnu). According to Odissi scholar-performer, Ratna Roy, Mahari dancing was a covert Tantric operation in an overt Vaishnavite program. Apffel Marglin denotes that the Mahari dance was a ritual offering to Jagannath, as an integral component of the Pancamakara ritual". (Urban, Power of Tantra, 102). According to the Shakta tradition or the worshipping of the Goddess, the Mahari dance was called Sakti Ucchista or the leavings of Kali or Sakti. The sexual connotations of Mahari dancing held primary importance in ensuring a healthy life-cycle in the Hindu ecosystem although they are completely obscured in the contemporary understanding of her ritual practice.

The confluence of the Jagannath cult with Vaishnavism around the sixteenth century led to the first instance of discrimination against the Mahari tradition as the Brahmin orthodoxy opposed the above life-affirming-sexually suggestive Tantric practices. Archaeologist Kishore Chandra Panigrahi claims the homogenizing influence of the Vaishnavite cult with the Bhakti movement that diminished the earlier religious influences in Odisha's religious fabric. In Jagannath cult, Jagannath is equated to Vishnu, who is also another form of Krishna. The Bhakti movement with its apparent democratizing impulse establishing a personalized relationship with Vishnu/ Krishna/ Jagannath became less tolerant of previous religious orders that incorporated the unorthodox Tantric practices. (Sarkar, Kaustavi, Mahari Out: Deconstructing Odissi).

At Ranipur Jharial, the Yogini images are large and all appear to be dancing, each with an identical pose. The positioning of the legs is fundamental to most Indian classical dance forms and is a stance assumed at the start of each set of movements. This is in contrast to the standing images of the Yoginis at Hirapur. The yogini images of Bheraghat temple, Madhya Pradesh are seated in Lalitasana. Dance and music have always been the significant activities associated with the Yoginis. Anamika Roy proceeds to describe Yoginis as 'tribal', their dancing movements as encoded within ritualistic magic, folkish secrecy and esotericism and finally as sexualised expression (p. 91- Anamika Roy, Sixty-Four Yoginis: Cult, Icons and Goddesses. xxv, 354 pp. New Delhi: Primus Books, 2015).

Referring to the typical Odissi dance iconography as exhibited by all Yogini images, C. Fabri writes:

Why do all the women dance here? Was dancing part of the esoteric practices carried out at dead of the night, in these arenas, combined with wine, meat and erotics? (As per the Bhavisyottara Purana, the invocation of the Yoginis always takes place at midnight on a new moon day.) *C.Fabri*

Dance, is a major form of portrayal for these aggressive energies called Yoginis. This dance of rage threatens the existence of the entire world. She is a symbol of the divine feminine, a fierce, shape shifting Tantric incarnate of the Cosmic Mother, a primitive animistic divinity, later absorbed into the cult of Shakti and Devi, worshipped between the 6th and 10th centuries in circular, roofless Tantric temples in groups of 64. The Yoginis of Ranipur Jharial have large, exaggerated physical traits which symbolise sensuality and fertility.

Her bare body the naked truth. Paired, in the dance of creation with the God of destruction, as Shiva and Shakti, she is said to embody energy, balance, the life force of existence,

Getting to know the Yoginis of Ranipur Jharial

The Chausathi Yogini temple at Ranipur Jharial is one of the two hypaethral temples of Odisha, (the other temple is located at Hirapur, near Bhubaneswar) significant with regard to its antiquity as well as its representation of the lost Tantra cult. By popular notion, it is believed that the hypaethral temples were constructed in dedication to deities of nature symbolizing fertility of the soil, of animals and of man.

The structure of this hypaethral temple is distinct from the Brahmanical or Buddhist temple structures. The temple is devoid of vimana or sikhara, mandapa or chambers, garbhagriha or sanctum. Locally the Chausathi Yogini temple of Ranipur-Jaharial is popularly referred to as 'Chakhar Badha' due to its circular shape.

A unique aspect of the Yogini statues at Ranipur Jharial is that all of them are dancing Yoginis, in different poses of the classical Odissi dance form, originating from Odisha. The theoretical foundations of Odissi can be traced to the ancient Sanskrit text Natya Shastra, its existence in antiquity evidenced by the dance poses in the sculptures of Hindu temples in Odisha, and archaeological sites of Hinduism,

Buddhism and Jainism. The statues in temples mostly show the *Samapada,* the *Tribhangi* and the *Chauka* of Odissi. The Ranipur Yoginis are all in the Samabhanga pose and show the "Bhangas" or body positions.

The inventory of the existing Yogini statues at Ranipur Jharial temple and details of vacant niches are provided here. Researchers have tried to name them by comparing them to descriptions in ancient, sacred texts and tantric literature and drawing similarities. References about the Chausathi Yoginis can be found in ancient scriptures like : Brahmananda Purana, Agni Purana, Skanda Purana, Kalika Purana, Jnanarnava Tantra, Brihad Nandikeswara Purana, Chandi Purana of Sarala Das, Brihndla Tantra, Bata Avakasa of Balaram Das, etc. Historical romances and semi-historical literature like Somadevasuri's Yasastilaka of AD 959, Kalhana's Rajatarangini of c.1150 and Somadeva's Kathasarit Sagara of c.1070 contain legendary stories about the all-powerful Yoginis.

An attempt has been made to name the Yogini statues, in keeping with their iconography and drawing similarities with the following existing lists:

Kalika Purana, Durgapuja Paddhati of Vrihannandikesvara Purana and Brihannila Tantra, Dr.Ramprasad Mishra research article.

1. Brahmi
(*Kalika Purana, Durgapuja Paddhati of Vrihannandikesvara Purana and Brihannila Tantra*)

A three headed two armed figure, she holds a trident on her left hand and a kumbha/

kamandalu on her right hand, resting on her left knee. It is probably the image of Brahmi or Brahmani, the Shakti of Brahma who according to Devi Mahatmya of Markandeya Purana has the swan as her vehicle and holds a kamandalu and aksasutra. She is a four-faced goddess, but her image here shows three faces because in accordance with the iconography of this deity one of her faces remains at the back.

2. Vacant - Belgar mentioned about the image that had originally been in this niche as "A two armed figure with a lotus in each hand, dancing on the pedestal of seven horses". *Cunningham describes her, more than a century ago as a unique statue with resemblance to the attributes of Surya, as holding a lotus in each of her two hands and as having seven horses depicted against her pedestal. (Dehejia, Yogini Cult and Temple- A Tantric Tradition.)*

3. Vacant – This niche had contained a two-armed figure, one hand holding a mace.

4. **Vidyutprabha**
(*Skanda Purana, Prabhasvara-Yoga-Varttika*)
This is a two-armed figure, single headed with her left hand on her naval in a typical posture of Odissi dance form, the right arm broken. It may be identified as the image of the Yogini Vidyutprabha who according to Tantric belief, illumines her body and invigorates her energy from her Navel-Plexus or Manipuraka Chakra.

5. Simhamukhi

(*Skandapurana and Tantric literature*)
She is a two armed lion headed figure, carrying a trident on her right hand and a cup in her left hand. It is possibly the image of Simhamuhki, whose description as a Yogini is found in Skandapurana and Tantric literature

6. Vrihatkusi

(*Skanda Purana*) : A two armed figure, holding a noose in her left hand, and a sword in her right hand. This image Vrihatkusi, as mentioned in the Skanda Purana.

7. A four-armed figure with all hands broken.

8. Vacant
9. Vacant
10. Vacant

11. A two armed figure, left hand on her left knee, right hand broken. This Yogini is described in ***Vrihat Nila Tantra*** and ***Sadabhichara Prayoganama Tantravallari.***

12. Maheswari

A three headed, four-armed figure. Upper right hand holds a trident and lower right hand is damaged. Upper left hand holds the rosary and lower left hand has been damaged.

13. Sukodari
(*Skanda Purana*)

A skeletal figure, right arm damaged, left arm on her cheek. As the image shows a shrinking belly, it may be assumed to be the image of Sukodari who is depicted in Skandapurana.

14. Vacant

15. A broken image (Belgar mentions it in niche number 14, and describes): "A six or eight armed image; with one pair of hands she is pulling her mouth wide, and with the remaining unbroken ones she holds an hour glass, a sword, a cup, and is dancing on a prostrate male figure". Cunnigham corroborates this observation. Her gesture of opening her mouth wide  indicates that she could be Yogini Attahasa, (the one who laughs loudly) or Yogini Hahavara (the one who utters loud sounds). It is presumed that it could be the image of Devi Parvati, the MahaYogini as its height and width is comparatively more compared to other Yoginis. It may have been placed in this niche at a later date after reshuffling of images in the cells. It is probable that this Parvati image was in front of Lord Shiva near the entrance.

16. **Bidali Devi**

Four armed figure with the head of a cat. The Yogini holds a club and sword in two hands, a skull-cap and a piece of flesh in the other two. This image is similar to Yogini Bidalidevi, meaning cat.

17. Hayagrva
(*Skandapurana*)
A horse headed figure, four armed, she holds in her unbroken hands a club, an hour glass and a rosary.

18. Ajasya Ajalochana
(*Pashu Prakashana Tantra*)
A goat-faced, four-armed image, holding a club in her left hand.

19. Vikatanana Vyaghrani
(*Skandapurana & Chausathi Yogini Namavali*)
A tiger headed, four-armed figure, carrying a bow (broken) in her upper left hand; in the upper right hand she holds an arrow and in the lower right hand a club. The lower left hand is broken.

20. Dhumanisvasa
(*Skanda Purana*)

A four armed deity, two hands folded on her chest, and the other two hands broken. It is probably the image of Yogini Dhumanisvasa who exhales smoke by pressing her chest with two hands and hypnotizes the victim by magical smoke. It is a war goddess and described as Yogini in the Skanda Purana.

21. Marjari
(*Skandapurana*)

A cat/leopard headed figure, four-armed; she is holding a sword in the upper right hand, and a human corpse by its legs with one of her left hands.

22. Gajananaa/Vainayaki
(*Skandapurana & Chaunsth Yogini Namavali*)

An elephant headed, four-armed figure, holding a battle axe in her upper left hand. The other hands are broken. The battle axe (symbolic of Ganesha) and elephant head connote that she could be Gajanana or Vainayaki.

23. **Varahi**
(*Skanda Purana, Chuansath Yogini Namavali and Brihat Nandikesvara Purana*)
A boar headed, four armed figure. With her upper right hand is carrying a club, and upper left hand, a rosary or mala. Adorned with a crown of a coiled snake, her other two hands are folded together in a Odissi dance mudra.

24. **Vrisanana**
(*Skandapurana*)
A bull headed, horned, four armed figure, with all hands broken.

25. A four armed figure, she has her upper right hand on her knee. Upper left hand lies on her breast. With her lower right hand she is holding a club and with lower left hand, a cup.

26. A four armed figure; the upper left hand is on her left ankle and lower left hand holds a rosary. The upper right hand is damaged.

27. **Riksasi**
(*Skandapurana*)
A four armed figure, all arms broken.

28. **Sarpasya**
(*Skandapurana*)
A serpent headed, four armed figure, one hand on her knee, another at her breast, the others holding a cup and a trident.

29. A two armed defaced figure with hands damaged.

30. A two armed figure, carrying a trident in her right hand, left hand damaged.

31. A two armed figure, with a distinct coiffure and traces of head jewellery.She has a benign expression.

32. Missing

33. **Prachanda**
(*Skanda Purana*)
A two armed figure, holding a trident in her right hand, left hand damaged.

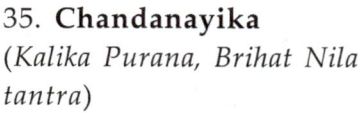

34. **Chhanda**
(*Brihat Nila Tantra, Kalika Purana*)
A two armed figure holding a cup in her left hand, right hand damaged.

35. **Chandanayika**
(*Kalika Purana, Brihat Nila tantra*)
A two armed figure holding a trident in her right hand and a cup in her left hand.

36. A two armed figure with both the hands broken.

37. **Chandogra**
(*Kalika Purana, Brihat Nila Tantra*)
A two armed figure carrying a trident in the right hand and a cup in her left hand.

38. **Ksemankari**
(*Kalika Purana*)
A four armed figure, carrying a trident in her upper right hand, a sword in upper left hand, with the lower left hand holding a cup. Closer scrutiny reveals a grotesque face, with sunken eyes and her hair decorated with a crown of skulls. It is probably the image of Ksemankari who is described as a Yogini in Kalika Purana.(Source: manuscript No. 345 of Odisha State Museum Library).

39. A two armed figure; both hands of this statue are damaged.

40. Vacant
41. Vacant

42. A stout two armed figure, holding a trident in her right hand. The left hand is broken.

43. **Sisighani**
(*Skandapurana*)
A two armed figure, holding a sword in the right hand and having a child on her knee.

44. **Sarabhanana**
(*Skanda Purana*)
A horse headed image of a four armed female. She holds a trident in one upper hand and a severed head by its hair in both lower hands.

45. **Pasahasta**
   (*Skanda Purana*)
   Yamaghanta
   (*Chaunsath Yogini Namavali*)

A two armed buffalo faced figure, holding a trident in her right hand, left hand damaged. It is probably the image of the Yogini Pasahasta or the arrester of the Jiva or life,

46. **Adya** (*Brihat Nila Tantra*)
   Yogesvari (*Chaunsath Yogini Namavali*)
   Brahma Vadini (*Brihat Nandikesvara Purana*)

A four armed figure, with the upper two hands joined over her head and lower two hands joined near her naval in a dancing posture. The figure is a symbolic indication of the yogic energisation of the naval plexus/MANIPURAKA CHAKRA and SAHASRARA CHAKRA/Cerebral plexus by using hands.

47. **Mrigasirsa**

(*Skandapurana*): Deer faced, two armed figure. On her right hand she holds a sword.

48. **Kotarinasika**

(*Skanda Purana*) : A two armed figure, holding a trident in her right hand, left hand damaged. The nose is slightly shrunk inwards, thus the name.

49. **Stulakeshi**

(*Skanda Purana*)

A two armed figure, her right hand is in the Abhaya mudra and left hand is on her knee. The deity has thick hair carved on her head.

50. Vacant

51. **Dantesukara**

(*Skanda Purana*)

This is a two armed figure in a distinct posture; she is rubbing her teeth with a finger of one of her hands as a toothbrush; the other holds what may be either a mirror or a cup.

52. **Sreshthini**

(*Chaunsath Yogini Namavali*)

A two armed figure, holding a club in her left hand. It is probably the icon of Sreshthini who confers affluence on the Sreshthins or the merchant class.

53. Vacant

54. **Bhayankari**

(*Brihat Nila Tantra*)

A four armed figure. Upper right hand holds a club. Lower left hand is broken.

55. **Indrani**
A four armed figure. Upper left hand holds a bow, upper right hand an arrow. Lower left hand holds a parasol and the lower right hand is damaged.

56. A two armed figure, holding a pair of pincers in the left hand; right hand is damaged.

57. A two armed figure, holding a noose in the right hand.

58. Vacant

59. **Vala Pramathini**
   (*Skanda Purana*)
A two armed figure, holding a club in right hand and a cup in the left hand. It is the image of Vala Pramathini whose weapons are noose and skull cup.

60. A two armed figure, one hand raised to her forehead. In the left hand she is holding a mirror. This is a typical dance pose of Odissi.

61. **Dandahasta**
(*Skanda Purana*)
A two armed figure, right hand holding a club.

62. Vacant
63. Vacant
64. Vacant

The Maze

Ancient Temples of Ranipur Jharial

The contribution of the Somavamsi dynasty to the history, cultural heritage, literature and language of Odisha in unparalleled. Often regarded as the builders of Odisha by historians, Somavamsis ruled for two hundred years. This period has been considered the golden era in the cultural heritage of Odisha. Kalinga, Utkala, Kongoda and Kosala were unified and brought under one political authority. The uniformity of administration facilitated a cultural synthesis leading to the emergence of a unique Odia culture. The Odisha temple architecture reached unimagined heights due to the patronage of the Somavamsis.

The Somavamsi rulers were devoted Shaivites and endeavoured to ensure the growth and promotion of Shaivism in Odisha by the construction of several Shiva temples and permitting generous sanctions of land grants to the Shaiva temples, priests and ascetics. Renowned Shaiva spiritual leaders, Sadasivacharya, Rathamacharya and Acharya Gaganasiva were invited to visit Odisha during their reign and enjoyed the patronage of the Somavamsi rulers. Supported by the patronage of Janmejaya I,

Gaganasiva supervised the construction of the Someswar temple at Ranipur Jharial. Copper plates that have been discovered indicate that Ranipur Jharial had been declared a sacred place of immense religious significance by Janmejay Mahabhavagupta who is also referred to as Kosalendra, the lord of Kosala. The group of temples at Ranipur-Jharial include few significant, monumental temples. Indralath, Chausathi Yogini and Someswara are unique for their outstanding archaeological finesse and monumental architecture.

The Temple cluster of Ranipur-Jharial can be classified on the basis of the architecture.
1. Somesvara Siva temple with an inscription on its lintel.
2. The hypaethral Chausathi Yogini temple.
3. The Indralath brick temple.
4. Two Khakhara temples.
5. Small stone temples.

Somatirtha

Somatirtha is an ancient name identified with the twin hamlets of Ranipur-Jharial in Balangir district of Odisha. Joseph David Beglar visited the temple town in 1874- 75. He was an Armenian-Indian engineer, archaeologist and photographer working in British India, reporting to ASI and was an assistant to Alexander Cunningham. He was deputed to several sites for his excellent photographic and negotiating skills. Around 1874-75, he was deputed to Bengal, Bihar and Odisha by Cunningham. Beglar documented the existence of a cluster of fifty-seven temples of various shapes and size. Most of these temples were in varying stages of decay even then. Beglar writes *"the occurrence of so many temples at this spot is sufficiently accounted for by the inscription which records the existence here of a tirth or place of pilgrimage"*. He stated the date of the structures to be 8th century A.D. and historian K.N. Mahapatra designated it between 650 to 950 A.D. Somatirtha, apparently, named after the presiding deity of this sacred shrine Somesvara Siva, finds mention in the Vamana Purana as noted by several historians. The existence of Somasagara, Somesvara Siva temple and a Visnu temple at Ranipur-Jharial further corroborates this contention. (Dr. C.B. Patel, Monumental Efflorescence of Ranipur-Jharial.) The temple cluster at Ranipur Jharial is named after these two villages located nearby. The site was referred to in ancient times as the Bhubaneswar of Daksina Kosala on account of the variety and number of temples grouped together there. The Vamana Purana, in its description of the holiest tirthas of medieval Odisha mentions it along with Viraja (Jajpur), Purusottama (Puri) and mount Mahendra. Pandit Kedarnath Mahapatra, Dr. N.K Sahu, and many other scholars of Odisha identified Ranipur-Jharial as Somatirtha- "The holy land of Soma".

These monuments were built when Tantricism gained prominence, with the allied and related background of Shaivism. This strain of Shaivism was not extreme, but leaned towards a composite and dynamic pluralistic model. It is evident that since 3rd or 4th century the place was known as a Shiva teertha. Shaivism was popular, being possibly a pre-Vedic cult which was accommodated in Vedic pantheon with increasing Sanskritization and mutual assimilation of features. Saivism was popular in ancient South Kosala and Kantara region (with tribal and Dravidian presence of populace) since the days of Nala dynasty. This is corroborated by excavations at Maraguda in Nawapara district where a Shaiva Vihara of circa $4/5^{th}$ century has been excavated. This Shaiva Vihara was ruthlessly destroyed, probably by Vakatakas or Sarabhapuriyas who were staunch Vaishnavites.

After being attacked and ruined, many adherants of Shaivism might have moved in the north-west direction from Maraguda and come to Ranipur-Jharial area where Shaivism might have already been prevalent. And Shaiva Tantric forces and traditions might have further gained momentum there.

Even though precise dating is difficult for these group of monuments, the accumulated artistic and architectonic acumen of the Post Gupta age seemed to have significant contribution to the building activities of this centre. David Beglar who visited this place in 1874-75 counted 57 temples of varied shapes and sizes at various stages of decay and preservation and noted the existence of 120 temples in early times.

Before this, the sway of Buddhism might have been prevalent. But as has been discussed earlier, the worship of mother goddess and Tantra predated Buddhism. The Buddhistic ways of Vajrayana and Sahajayana etc. developed in Odisha because of the presence and prevalence of the Tantric cults prior to it. Hence there has been a mystic tradition that has assumed the garb of Jainism, Buddhism and Hinduism (with its Shaivite, Vaishnavite and mixed liberal traditions) and in the process modified and sometimes eroded itself. But it was there prior to all these major streams of religion and its origin in lost in the mists of historical antiquity.

Chausathi Yogini temple

The Chausathi yogini (64 yogini temple) temple is an exceptional architectural monument situated at Ranipur Jharial. There are two Yogini temples identified with the

Sakta religion in Odisha located at Ranipur Jharial and Hirapur, Khurda respectively. The Chausathi yogini temples were the seat of Yogini cult, the Tantrik form of Shaivism. Sadasivacarya and Gaganasivacarya were priests of the Mattyamayuri School who contributed significantly to the propagation of the Yogini cult in South Kosala during the Somavamsi period. (E.I., Vol. XXIV. PP.239-243). Both were followers of Matsyendranath and worshipped Kalabhairava, a tantrik form of Siva and Yogini, the consort of Kalabhairava.

Chausathi Yogini Temple, Ranipur Jharial

A hypaethral temple, Ranipur-Jharial Chausathi Yogini shrine has a unique ground plan. (Senapati, N, ed, op.cit, P.492) It measures 54.44 feet diameter in the outer portion and 44.60 feet in the interior portion. The height of the wall is 8.86 feet and consists of five courses of hammer-dressed stone as hard masonry. The passage of entry to the shrine measures 5.18 feet in width and 5.74 feet in length. The interior area of the shrine has 64 carved niches as the seat of the Yogini images. T.E. Donaldson estimated the period of construction of this temple as the early part of 10th Century C. E. during the reign of the Somavamsi dynasty in Odisha.

Leharigudi

Built in the Khakhara style of architecture, this ancient shrine is in a dilapidated condition. The name of the temple could have been derived from Luipa, a tantric Siddha. Constructed on the banks of the Someswar Sagar, the temple has striking similarities with Vaital Deul of Bhubaneswar with regard to style and design. Research indicates that the rudimentary temple architecture of this Sakta shrine, is indicative of a time-line close to the 5th or beginning of the 6th century A.D. Similar temple structures that are lost have left behind impressions of the glorious epoch of the area.

Someswar Temple

This temple is in a good state of preservation, compared to other ruined temples in this cluster. There is an inscription by Ganganasiva, the celebrated Shaivite, here which reads *"Somasvami Siddhesvara Laxminama Chaturthanam"*. Among several images of Gods and Goddesses, there are unique images of Durga. Vrisabha,

Nagi and a Dwarapala. The image of Gajalakshmi is found on the lintel of the entrance to the Garbhagriha of the temple. A distinct inscription of a deity who could be Buddha or Siddha in dhyana-mudra is found on the entrance wall and in the sanctum sanctorum, the linga symbolizing Someswar is found.

Someswar Temple, image
Source: http://ignca.gov.in/online-digital-resources

Someswar Temple, image
Source: http://ignca.gov.in/online-digital-resources

Ranipur Mound, Ranigudi

The name of the site, "Ranipur Jharial" might have been derived from the term Ranigudi or Ranipur (Queen's Palace). There is popular belief that the Queen's palace might have been located in close proximity to the temple. The Ranod inscription of Madhya Pradesh mentions Ranipadra, which may be the earlier name of present day Ranipur. According to ancient belief, Ranipur was the place where the queens of Patnagarh used to stay. Jharial used to be a fort.

Indralath Brick Temple

It is a unique brick temple, described by different researchers and historians as either a Siva or Vishnu temple. Considered to be the tallest temple in Odisha, it is one of the few surviving ancient temples of Balangir, Odisha. The Shikhara, almost 60 feet high is erected on a high sand – stone platform. In the temple there are distinct images of Shiva-Parvati, Ganesh etc. The water channel tapering out from the linga is considered to be the original one.

Indralath Temple, Ranipur Jharial

Historians have varying viewpoints regarding when and by whom the temple was constructed. One of the three namely the Nala dynasty, Panduvamshis of Dakshina Kosala and Somavamshi dynasty who ruled over Odisha and Chhattisgarh between the 6th – 12th century could be credited with its construction. This ancient brick temple was featured on stamp by India Post for its remarkable combination of architecture and craftsmanship.

The architects and patrons of the famous Indralath brick temple and the hypaethral temple of Chausathi Yoginis have not been definitely ascertained. Beglar and Williams suggest it to belong to the 7th century. A detailed and comprehensive survey of art and architecture of South Kosala and specifically, Ranipur-Jharial during the specified period reveals that there was an unprecedented level of artistic activities in this region. Belief in various gods and goddesses of many pantheons encouraged the rulers of this region to reflect them through the medium of stone carvings. The affluence of the kingdom as well as the generous patronage and enthusiasm of the rulers created an ideal climate for artistic excellence. Ranipur-Jharial may be regarded as a temple town of significant importance in the remote past.

This rare brick structure is a symbol of the great architectural skill of the craftsmen of South Kosala. Perched atop an elevated platform, it is a towering edifice, probably the highest brick temple among its prototypes in the upper Mahanadi valley in ancient South Kosala. The bricks which are used in this temple are generally 14 inches in length, seven inches in breadth Cuboid in size, these bricks are well designed and strong. Pancharatha in style of architecture it consists of a vimana and a Jagamohana. The garbhagriha stands supported by four stone pillars in its four corners. The ceiling is carved with a beautifully designed lotus on the inner roof of the temple. Sculptural carving of the lotus on the ceiling of this temple not only magnifies its beauty but also adds to its religious importance as a sacred symbol. The superb masonry skills exhibit the advanced scientific techniques in architecture. The Indralath brick temple of Ranipur is truly a gem of the cultural excellence of South Kosala.

Indralath Temple, Ranipur Jharial

Even as the construction of temples is by stones in majority of cases, there have been temples made of bricks and clay in eastern and central India. There are brick and clay temples in Bishnupur of Bengal. There are many such temples in the Kosala region, in Striper (now in Chhattisgarh). In Odisha, there are quite a few brick temples, especially, in the Prachee Valley bordering Puri and Cuttack districts, though the temples are much smaller compared to the Indralath Temple.

The most important figure of Ranipur Jharial is that of Varaha incarnation of Lord Vishnu carved on a huge rocky elevation of ten feet in height and twenty-five feet in length, situated on the south-eastern embankment of the Samiabandh tank. A profile figure of four-handed Varaha of the height of around four feet and breadth of two feet and a half is carved on this huge boulder. The Lord is seen wearing Aksamala or beads of Rudraksa as Hara, Keyura, Kankana and Katibandha. In his lower left and right hands, he is seen holding Sankha and Gada respectively, while in his upper right hand there is Cakra. The upper left hand of this figure is powerful and vigorous. Varaha is seen touching the left portion of his chest with folded palm and holding on his elbow the seated figure of Bhudevi like a child. His left leg is slightly raised and placed on the chest of Adisesa, whose figure is human above and snake below waist. Here the Naga Adisesa is seen to be having a five-hooded snake canopy on his head and is having both his hands folded in obeisance to the Lord in Anjali pose. He is worshipfully looking at the great deliverer of the earth with uplifted head. This serpent, Adisesa is accompanied by his wife, a Nagini, up-waist in human form under a five-hooded snake-canopy and below waist in snake form seen to be entwined with the snake form of her male counterpart. Her right hand is firmly placed on the ground with the support of which this Nagini is sitting. Her left arm is raised up. It is a unique figure of BhuVaraha, carved on the body of a rocky elevation. No such figure is found else-where in the entire upper Mahanadi valley of Orissa. (Panda, S.S, The Rock-cut carvings of the upper Mahanadi Valley).

The destination has immense potential for niche tourism. But most of these rare temples are in a dilapidated condition and need immediate care and attempts for preservation. The Yogini temple is regarded as an important shrine of a lost cult and needs to be preserved. Unfortunately, 13 of the 64 structures of yoginis made up of sandstone are missing and in need immediate conservation.

Indralath Temple, Ranipur Jharial

The place is surrounded by other historically important sites like Nrusinghanath, Maraguda, Podagarh, Asurgarh, Belkhandi, Saintala and Patnagarh.

The cluster of temples at Ranipur Jharial showcases different architectural styles like rekha, khakara, pidha and hypaethral. The material used for construction are granite, sandstone, and bricks. According to the Ancient Monuments and Archaeological Sites and Remains Act, 1958, ancient monuments or archaeological sites and remains, as the case may be, which are of historical, archaeological or artistic interest, and have been in existence for not less than 100 years, are declared by the Central Government as that of national importance.

The protection and maintenance of monuments, declared as of national importance, is taken up by the ASI by way of structural repairs, chemical preservation and environmental development around the monument, which is a regular and ongoing process and the required works are taken-up on need basis as per the established principles of conservation, subject to availability of resources, as per the ASI website.

In addition, the monuments of national importance are ensured tourist-related amenities such as drinking water, toilet blocks, facilities for physically challenged, pathways, cultural notice boards/signage, vehicle parking, cloakrooms among others.

Standing at the monument site that serene evening with the canvas of the sky glowing radiant, one can feel the pulse of this mysterious Yogini temple! The ambience seems animated, the Chausathi Yogini statues come alive, as it were, the past joining the present in a loop of time and the place unfolds tales untold, in its own sphinx-like silence!

The untapped tourism potential of Ranipur Jharial

The cult of sixty-four Yoginis was the exuberant expression of an extreme form of tantrism in about 8th century A.D. when the occult and esoteric Sadhana reached an unprecedented height. Over time, the cult lost its sway and was forgotten along with its temples spread across India and the rare statues they contained. The Yogini Cult is essentially a celebration of womanhood, symbolizing the worship of the feminine force. The temple is the focus for the myriad dimensions of everyday life - religious, cultural, educational and social. The temple is also the place where one can wish to transcend the mundane world of man.

The psychology of tourist behaviour is greatly shaped by the psychological, cultural and social factors. Psychological factors include the interplay of various motivational forces like self-actualization, esteem, perception, ego transactions, loyalty etc. However, each travel group has its own culture influencing its buying behaviour which differs greatly from country to country.

The new age traveller is in search of authentic experiences. Researchers have argued that New Age spirituality is best understood as a form of 'self-spirituality' and as an expression of the consumer capitalist tendency to commodify all things, in the process converting religion into a 'spiritual marketplace'. (Ivakhiv). Odisha is successfully promoting its temples as destinations for temple tourism. Efforts must be directed to promote the Chausathi Yogini temples, both at Hirapur and Ranipur Jharial at Odisha as tourism destinations of importance, both rare cultural tourism destinations, seats of the lost Yogini cult. The spiritual tourists who visit these destinations have varied travel motivations, sometimes having no religious affiliation to the destination or Goddesses. There is perhaps no place in Odisha and even India which is more identifiable with a secluded cult shrouded in mystery and spirituality. The glorious and ancient spiritual culture of the Yogini cult has drawn pilgrims, seekers, and philosophers from all around the world. But what really makes this spiritual destination unique is that notwithstanding the religion one adheres to, there is a spiritual experience awaiting the traveller. All the same, the takeaway varies, from the existential tourist to the backpacker, the ritualist to the sightseer.

Despite, war, terrorism, natural calamities and other major hindrances to travel and tourism and the most recent tragedy by the pandemic, the tourism industry continues to flourish in several niche sectors. It is resilient and has the tendency to spring back, especially in different forms of alternative tourism. Alternative tourism is travel that is personal, authentic and facilitates interaction with the local culture, people and communities. The global community has been particularly interested in the "developing world" for authentic yet uncommon experiences. An increasing number of world-travellers are in the pursuit of spiritual transformation in "less developed" locales of the world.

There has been a noticeable onset of Tantra Tourism among new-age travellers. From seeking one's identity to redefining leisure, the Nirvana- driven tourist finds Tantra Tourism to be a wondrous pursuit. Tantra is an ancient Indian spiritual practice, grossly misrepresented as an offshoot of backpacker or religious tourism. From the search for magic, mystery of tantric yoga to countercultural seekers, Tantric Tourism has become a global pursuit. The new breed of travellers are travellers by choice, educated and adhering to unconventional beliefs.

Tour operators offer hand-crafted tours to these destinations in ways to embody the 'sacred feminine' even without tourists knowing much about tantric traditions. The consumption of tantric-related tourism products is facilitated through pilgrimages to 'festivals' organized at these destinations (The Chausathi Yogini Festival at Hirapur).

There are several theories about the motivations of religious and pilgrimage tourists. Urry's three-tier typology of tourist co-presence includes: face-to-face, face-the-place, and face-the-moment. Face-to-face refers to the intense commingling which facilitates feelings of interconnectedness. Face-the-place refers to physically walking, seeing, touching, doing, and being, etc., which is a self-evident part of pilgrimage. Face-the-moment refers to the 'timing' of travelling to and being at a 'live' event. Wanderlust is a perfect example of a globalised, syndicated festival, which occurs in several locations around the world, offering an 'endless summer of yoga', in which it becomes the context for 'conscious living'. (McCartney Patrick, Yoga-scapes, Embodiment and Imagined Spiritual Tourism September 2019).

Driven by consciousness motivations, women solo travellers move around alone in the pursuit of adventure, independence, feeling of personal fulfilment, individuality and escape. The women tourist's motivations for independent travel and tourism experiences are related to the desire to learn, self-development, challenge themselves, find a sense of identity and autonomy, meet new people and experience new life and adventure moments. These motivate solo women travel experiences (Pereira & Silva, 2018). On the other hand, young women may be travelling more because they have greater freedom and choice arising from greater economic, social, and leisure independence.

All these niche tourist segments can be directed to the Tantra circuit of Odisha. One of the rare destinations for Tantra/Spiritual/Religious Tourism is Ranipur Jharial in Bolangir district of Western Odisha. Situated in the green environs of the Titilagarh sub-division in Bolangir district, the twin villages of Ranipur- Jharial bear strong traces of their very old heritage. Ranipur Jharial is located in the Titilagarh (also spelt Titlagarh) subdivision of Bolangir district. Titilagarh was the Taitala Janapada which finds mention in Panini's Astadhyayi. During the time of Grammarian Panini (5th Century B.C), a place called Taitila Janapada flourished to the west of Kalinga, identified by historians with the modern town of Titlagarh in Balangir district. Taitala Janapada was famous for trade in some commodities described as "Kadru" the meaning of which may be either horse or cotton fabrics. Titlagarh is the nearest town, close to the historical site of Ranipur Jharial. In Titlagarh town there is a beautiful hill, Kumuda Pahad, offering a panoramic view of the town and its surrounding villages and forest areas with caves in it. There are reportedly the remnants of a tunnel joining a cave in these hills with

Ranipur Jharial. It is interesting to note that the capital of the Somavanshi and other kings ruling the region had shifted from Sonepur to Titilagarh and subsequently to Ranipur Jharial, before finally moving to Patnagarh.

A tourist circuit could be developed with the town of Titilagarh along with destinations like Maraguda, Harishankar, Turekela, Bhima Dunguri, Jogisarada, Saintala, and Belkhandi etc. to create an attractive itinerary for tourists visiting Ranipur Jharial. There is a hill trekking track connecting Harishankar to Gandhamardan Hills which can be developed as a route for adventure and eco-tourism. These shall have a positive synergy or cluster effect along with religious or cultural niche tourism. Nrusinghnath and Harishankar in the northern and southern sides of the Gandhamardan Hills are beautiful, natural spots with falls and fine temples. These sites could be included in the tourism circuit to be developed or augmented in and around Ranipur Jharial. Gandhamardan hills is home to 70% of the species of medicinal herbs found in India. It is also the habitat of a few rare species of fauna.

The twin temples representing the Yogini Cult in Odisha, the Chausathi Yogini temples at Hirapur and Ranipur Jharial are potential niche tourism destinations. Religious and spiritual tourists, solo travellers, and special interest tourists frequent this circuit. Shaivism, Vaishnavism, Buddhism and Tantrism clearly wielded an immense deal of influence in the region and this. essentially is a point of attraction for Tantra practitioners. The Chausathi Yogini temple at Ranipur Jharial has been declared to be of national importance and protected under the Ancient Monument and Archaeological Sites and Remains Act 1958 (24) of 1958.

Despite being one of the largest single temple

complexes of India, Ranipur Jharial has yet not received adequate attention. Art historians have not shown sufficient interest because these temples do not offer much scope for architectural study. Similarly, scholars working in the field of religious history, especially Shaiva-Sakta tradition have referred to the Chausathi-Yogini temple as one of the rarest shrines of India, but nobody has ever tried to situate Ranipur-Jharial in the broader context of South-Kosala's regional tradition on the one hand and the growing religious complexities and the emergence of temples on the other.

The Chausathi Yogini Mahotsav is an annual festival of performing arts hosted at the famed heritage site of 64-Yogini temple at Hirapur. It is a crowd-puller with a number of captivating performances. Similar events can be planned and organized at Ranipur Jharial to ensure greater tourist footfall to ensure renewed interest in this lost cult.

Temples constitute a significant symbol of art and architecture reflecting an amalgamated essence of spiritualism, religious belief, and culture. Referred to as Devalaya, Shivalaya, Devayatana etc., in the contemporary world, temple tourism is regarded to be a component of special interest tourism. It can also be packaged as an augmented tourism product paired with other tourism resources like cultural, heritage, religious, and spiritual tourism, art and architecture, fairs and festivals etc.

The following tour operators offer specially designed tours for Ranipur Jharial.

Department of Tourism

Balangir is an important commercial city with a rich cultural heritage. The place is famous for its beautiful setting with many old temples and shrines and the indigenous tribes that dwell here since time immemorial. Balangir in

Odisha is proud of its rich cultural heritage. A planned township established way back in 1871, Balangir was once a tiny hamlet until Ram Chandra Deo III made it his capital. Famous as the cultural hub of Western Odisha, particularly for its indigenous tribe Kosali's folk art and dance, Balangir is known for its temperate climate and many temples, parks, picnic spots, age-old buildings and the famous Sambalpuri cotton fabric. Destinations include Bhima Dunguri, Kumuda Pahad, Turekela, Ranipur Jharial, Pataneswari Temple, Harishankar etc)
(https://www.orissatourism.org/balangir-destination-guide)

- TourTravelWorld.com
- Le Magique Tantra Tours
- Travel Link Private Limited
- OTDC
- Heritage Tours Orissa
- Inspirock.com
- Theindiantrip.com
- Elicitodisha.com

However, despite having the potential to be an exclusive destination, it is largely unexplored, less travelled to and utterly neglected. Most of the temples are in a dilapidated state and need immediate attention and intervention of the government as well as the archaeologists for preservation. Inadequate protection of the huge complex can lead to looting and pilferage. Many locals and tourists take their vehicles right up to the top of the rocky outcrop where the ruins of Ranipur Jharial lie despite strict instructions not to take vehicles beyond a certain point. Picnickers throng and litter the place. Archaeological Survey of India (ASI) is entrusted with conserving the site. Except few signboards of ASI that declare the monuments as protected, there are no other noticeable activities of the

ASI. The destination has tremendous potential to provide participants or tourists to be immersive travellers where they can be a part of the culture, lifestyle and other activities related to the locals there. If developed and maintained properly, this destination can attract foreign tourists including scholars and researchers. Provision of proper amenities and building up of an ambience and interest in the place and its vibes shall go a long way in restoring its long lost glory as a hub of culture, as it was in the days of yore.

Collectives of female deities have a long-standing significance in history, mythology, legend and the natural landscape. Not only the temple but a great variety of heritage assets are scattered in and around the temple complex, which are inadequately maintained and require attention. Lack of awareness about the religious significance of the site has made it a leisure spot, with activities endangering the sanctity of the place. The identification of the heritage resources, ascertaining their value and significance as they exist now, as well as the development and implementation of important mitigation methods to improve the site need to be taken up urgently. An attempt to rekindle interest in the sacred geometry, history, architectural style, art forms, rich iconography details and rituals mentioned in the mythological text needs to be taken up. The site faces certain number of footfall as of now and requires proper management of the destination for the visitors. The Yogini circuit of Odisha can generate interest in the international tourism market. Tourism stakeholders and promoters should be actively involved for packaging the destination to facilitate tourists' influx. Better infrastructure, easy accessibility of domestic as well as international tourists can be ensured to this ancient seat of a fascinating cult. The state tourism department should develop unique promotional platforms for Ranipur Jharial as a rare, ancient destination. A well-planned marketing strategy blending with local cultural fairs and festivals will definitely attract tourists.

The pulse of this sacred space, the power of the Yoginis can only be felt by the one who truly searches for them. The infinite wisdom of the ages and the sacred creative force of All that is, will be and ever was is felt as one walks towards the dancing Yoginis. When one visits this sacred and solitary spot on a serene day, one feels as if the Yoginis ache to express a longing for the long-lost legacy, the past joining the present in a loop of time, yet again, and a song emerges from silence echoing the Yogini's seeking of Shiva, the yearning for the eternal and the infinite!

Shiva,
You inhabit me like a wreathe of sadness
Coiled all over me and deep inside
Ever since you left, countless aeons ago!
Except you, Shiva
No one knows of the life ember flickering in me
Almost dead, in the throes of killing pain
Beneath the mute stony surface, the wind ravaged face
Beneath thousand covers of Time
I am alive, even now.
Will you not come again, Shiva?
And repaint me with your intense colors,
Perch me on the highest boughs of love
The waiting wearies me
Come, we will enact our roles
Yet again.
(Yogini Poems: Love and Life by Adyasha Das)

References

Agrawal, S, Kosala Itihas O Anyanya Prabandha

Brighenti Francesco, Sakti Cult in Orissa

Comprehensive History and Cultural History and Culture of Orissa, Editor J. K. Samal, P. K. Mishra.

Choudhury, Dr. Janmejay, Origin of Tantricism and Sixty-Four Yogini Cult in Orissa.

Das, Adyasha : Chausathi Yoginis of Hirapur- from Tantra to Tourism

Das, D.R. Temples of Orissa

Dehejia, Vidya 1986, pp. 103-114.

Donaldson. Tantra and Sakta Art of Orissa, Vol. III,

E.I.,Vol.XXIV. PP.239-243

Govindarajan, Hema; The Nataraja Image from Asanpat, article published in Dimensions of Indian ArtPupul Jayakar Seventy', Vol.I, ed. by Lokesh Chandra and Yotindra Nath, Agam Kala Prakashan, Delhi, 1986, p.145.)

Hatley, Shaman (2007). The Brahmayamalatantra and Early Saiva Cult of Yoginis. University of Pennsylvania (PhD Thesis, UMI Number: 3292099).

Hatley, Shaman :What is a yogini? Towards a polythetic definition

Keul, Istvan: Yogini's in South Asia

Patel, C.B. Monumental Efflorescence of Ranipur-Jharial in

Orissa Review, August 2004, pp.41-44 Archived 30 September 2007 at the Wayback Machine.

Rajguru, S.N., Inscription of Orissa

Rao, T.A. Gopinatha, Elements of Hindu Iconography, Vol.II, Part-I, Indological Book House, Varanasi, 1971 (Second Edition), pp.223-231 ff.

Roy Anamika, Sixty-Four Yoginis: Cult, Icons and Goddesses. xxv, 354 pp. New Delhi: Primus Books, 2015.

Royo, Lopez Alessandra," Guru Surendranath Jena: Subverting the Reconstituted Odissi Canon, Dance Matters

Senapati, N,.ed, op.cit, P.492

Seth, Dr.N. Ranipur Jharial: The Most Notable Monument in Western Odisha, IJMDRR

http://ignca.gov.in/online-digital-resources

Wikipedia/ blog.britishmuseum.org

www.sahasa.in

BLACK EAGLE BOOKS

www.blackeaglebooks.org
info@blackeaglebooks.org

Black Eagle Books, an independent publisher, was founded as a nonprofit organization in April, 2019. It is our mission to connect and engage the Indian diaspora and the world at large with the best of works of world literature published on a collaborative platform, with special emphasis on foregrounding Contemporary Classics and New Writing.

www.ingramcontent.com/pod-product-compliance
Lightning Source LLC
Chambersburg PA
CBHW071249070526
44583CB00017B/2397